# WHAT IF IT'S TRUE?

# WHAT IF IT'S TRUE?

## Unleashing the Power of the Resurrection in Your Life

# RAY JOHNSTON

THRIVE PUBLICATIONS
GRANITE BAY, CALIFORNIA

*What If It's True?*

Published by Thrive Publications
    PO Box 2336
    Granite Bay, CA 95746

Cover design: Tim Chambers and David Durham

First printing, 2006

Printed in the United States of America

ISBN 0-9779306-0-2

## *To my kids:*
## *Mark, Scott, Christy, and Leslie*

You invaded our lives, and for 18 years your soccer, volleyball, basketball, homework, guitars (and more guitars), hamsters, stray cats, small fish, big horses, lost dogs, found Christmas scavenger presents, vacations, homework, broken bones, trampolines, and Kings games have caused laughter to echo off our walls. Of all the kids in the world, Mom and I would choose you! You have always been fun to hang out with and a joy to parent. I love you.

## ACKNOWLEDGMENTS

A FRIEND OF MINE TELLS THE STORY about a man who entered his donkey into the Kentucky Derby. When questioned, he replied, "Oh, I don't expect him to win, but I thought the association would do him good." During this project, I have enjoyed the association of some world-class people. To a few of them, I would like to express my appreciation.

TO PROJECT COORDINATOR SARAH BENTLEY— Your energy, class, and positive spirit consistently turn work into fun. Your laughter and joy are contagious. You are England's best export to America. I'll thank the queen next time I see her.

TO MY CO-WRITER, BOB SMIETANA— You are a talented writer, thinker, and editor. And during this project you have consistently gone the extra mile. Thanks for everything.

TO DARLENE ANDERSON— Your faithfulness to the cause of Christ and loyalty to me and Bayside continue to inspire me and the community.

TO PAUL CARROLL— Your editing brilliance is coupled with a genuine love for God and people. You have the gift of making everything and everyone better.

TO MY LONGTIME ASSISTANT, CINDY UHLER— I am still not sure how you get it all done. Bayside would not be at the level it is without you. Neither would I.

TO LINCOLN BREWSTER— Knowing you are leading worship makes me break the speed limit driving to church. You are the best!

TO DAVID DURHAM, TIM CHAMBERS, KERRY SHEARER, AND JOHN VOLINSKY— Four guys who make the impossible happen regularly. The care and excellence you bring honor God.

*Continued...*

# ACKNOWLEDGMENTS

To Phil Sommerville, Jeri Mann, Patty Lauterjung, and Denise Belden— Your writing, thoughts, and support have been invaluable.

To the Bayside Staff— I am convinced that God looked down and said, "I'd better surround Ray with really good people." He has. No pastor has had the privilege of working with a finer group of people.

To the Bayside Leadership Team— I am grateful for your commitment to Christ, your care and concern for me and my family, and your diligent oversight of the ministries of our Family of Churches.

To the Bayside Church Family— The last two years have been amazing. One new building. Four new service times. Five new orphanages. Eight new church plants. Thousands of people becoming Christians. An $18,000,000 new capital campaign.... And the same old pastor. God has been so good to us, it's embarrassing. Being one of the pastors at Bayside continues to be an honor for which I thank God every single day.

To the pastors of the Bayside Family of Churches: Jim Holst, Sherwood Carthen, Leonard Lee, Chuck Wysong, Ed Kemp, Donnie Burleson, John Witham, and Cary Brooks— Your faith in God and commitment to improve our region continue to motivate me. I look forward to years of serving Christ together.

And to my wife, Carol— I will be forever grateful that God allowed me to marry my best friend. Thanks for everything!

# CONTENTS

# CONTENTS

# FOREWORD

WHEN I WAS 21 YEARS OLD, a group of Christians challenged me to discredit the claims of Christianity. Having discounted them all my life, I figured the challenge would be easy. After all, I thought, one needed to check his brains at the door of most churches. Applying a little reason should make the claims disappear.

I decided the fastest way to do away with the claims of the Christian faith would be to discredit the Resurrection of Jesus Christ. I began there. However, the more I studied, the more I uncovered historical, overwhelming evidence for the existence of Christ and for the Resurrection. That discovery not only led me to a personal relationship with Jesus Christ but took me on a lifelong journey, writing and speaking around the world about the Resurrection and its impact on our lives.

In *What If It's True?*, Ray Johnston explores 30 practical ways that the Resurrection changed the lives of the early Christians and can transform us today. You will be challenged as you discover how the truth of the Resurrection can change your life.

It is my prayer that this book will help you to experience the power and presence of God. You'll find, as I did, that there is no better way to live.

—JOSH MCDOWELL

# INTRODUCTION
### *Something happened in that room...*

I GREW UP IN A FAMILY OF SKEPTICS. We doubted every-thing. Reading books like *Inherit The Wind*, I assumed there was little evidence for the existence of God and even less for the validity of the Christian faith. My spiritual cynicism was so hardened that I actually talked a friend out of becoming a Christian.

Finally, I took an honest look at the evidence (summarized in Chapter 31). Much to my surprise, after a six-month investigation I found that the evidence for the historical reliability of the Resurrection was compelling. I completely lost my lack of faith.

Even more to my surprise, I discovered that I wasn't just making an intellectual decision. I was also unleashing in my life the kind of transforming power that we're all striving to find.

One of my favorites stories will explain this: Scott and Leslie Holst were on their honeymoon and arrived in the wee hours of the morning at a fancy hotel. Excited, they were looking forward to spending their first night together in a luxurious bed in the hotel's bridal suite. When they got to their room, they found a sofa, chair, and table but no bed. After several minutes, they discovered the sofa was a hide-a-bed. They spent a fitful night tossing and turning on a lumpy mattress and sagging springs.

Their honeymoon night ruined, the next morning Scott stormed down to the front desk and gave the clerk a tongue-lashing. "There must be some mistake," the clerk said, after checking the Holsts' reservation. "Didn't you open the door to the bedroom?"

Scott went back up to the room, opened the door that he thought led to a closet, and discovered the bedroom to the bridal suite. Inside was a king-sized bed covered with fruit baskets, boxes of chocolates, and a dozen red roses. Completely available yet totally unused.

Some doors are too important to leave closed! This book is an invitation to open the door to the implications of the Resurrection and its power in your life.

The early Christians spent the first Easter Sunday morning behind a locked door. They huddled together, fearing for their lives. Jesus had just been killed, and they thought they were next. They walked into that room defeated. But when they walked out, they were dynamic. They walked into that room crushed. They walked out confident. They walked in having a pity party. They walked out ready to take on the world. They walked into that room paralyzed by fear. They walked out filled with faith. Something happened in that room.

What happened? That's what this book is about. Join me for the next 31 chapters, and you can experience the same kind of transformation that the disciples underwent that first Easter.

I hope you'll find this book so compelling that you'll want to read it in one sitting, but I suggest taking it one chapter at a time. Many of you will go even further, gathering a few friends and using this book as a way of helping each other enjoy the power of God. However you read and use this book, I pray you'll experience the same power I've discovered. Now, open the door and unleash the power of the Resurrection in your life.

*Because of the Resurrection...*

# 1

# You Can Develop a Confident Faith

*Jesus replied, "I tell you the truth, if you have faith and do not doubt, not only can you do what was done to the fig tree, but also you can say to this mountain, 'Go, throw yourself into the sea,' and it will be done."*

Matthew 21:21

A STORY IS TOLD about a pastor in northern Wisconsin. The lack of pastors in the area meant he often traveled to small rural communities to do funerals. He usually traveled with the undertaker, driving in the undertaker's hearse. Once, on the way back from a funeral, the exhausted pastor decided to take a nap. Since they were in a hearse, he lay down in the back. Running low on fuel, they pulled into a service station. As the station attendant filled the tank, he was rather freaked out, because he noticed a body stretched out in the back. Just as the attendant was finishing, the pastor woke up, opened his eyes, knocked on the window, and waved at the attendant. He later said he'd "never seen anybody run so fast in his whole life!" **When people see life where they are expecting death—this causes a reaction!**

None of the disciples expected life on Easter Sunday, especially one of my favorite people in the Bible, Thomas. He's gotten a bad rap in the church. We call him "Doubting Thomas" and mock his lack of faith. But growing up in a "show me the evidence" family, I respect Thomas because I like his honesty.

Put yourself in his shoes for a minute. He wasn't with the other disciples when Jesus first appeared to them on Easter. When they told him, "We've seen the Lord," Thomas found that a little hard to swallow. "Unless I see the nail marks in His hands and put my finger where the nails were and put my hand into His side," he said, "I will not believe it." (JOHN 20:25)

Here's what Thomas was really saying: "I followed Jesus for three years. I heard His words and saw His miracles. I believed in Him, but now He's dead. And I will not believe He's alive unless I see Him with my own eyes." Thomas wasn't about to settle for a second-hand faith and a second-hand God. He wanted a faith with reasons; one that had its foundation on fact. Thomas was saying he would follow Jesus, if and only if he was convinced Jesus was alive!

For Thomas, and those of us like him, proof of the Resurrection is essential. After all, who needs a dead Savior!

A week later, Thomas got what he asked for. Jesus appeared to the disciples. "Put your finger here; see My hands," Jesus told Thomas. "Reach out your hand and put it into My side. Stop doubting and believe."

Jesus once told His disciples that if they had faith, and did not doubt, they would be able to move mountains. After the Resurrection, that's exactly what the disciples did. They traveled the world, testifying that Jesus had risen from the grave. Within 300 years, even the Roman emperor would kneel down and worship Jesus.

Thomas put aside his doubt and lived for Jesus. He knew that his faith in Christ was not in vain. The same cannot be said for famed writer and philosopher George Bernard Shaw. Toward the end of his life, he wrote: "The science to which I pinned my faith is bankrupt. Its counsels, which should have established the millennium, led instead directly to the suicide of Europe. I believed them once. In their name I helped to destroy the faith of millions of worshippers in the temples of a thousand creeds. And now they look at me and witness the great tragedy of an atheist who has lost his faith."

Stop doubting and believe.

*Because of the Resurrection...*  2

# YOU CAN RECEIVE ETERNAL LIFE

*"For it is by grace you have been saved, through*
*faith—and this not from yourselves, it is the gift of*
*God, not by works, so that no one can boast."*
EPHESIANS 2:8-9

A veteran Sunday school teacher tells this story:

"If I sold my house and my car, had a big garage sale and gave all my money to the church, would that get me into heaven?" I asked the children in my Sunday school class.

"No!" the children all answered.

"If I cleaned the church every day, mowed the yard, and kept everything neat and tidy, would that get me into heaven?"

Again, the answer was, "No!"

"Well, then, if I was kind to animals and gave candy to all the children, and loved my wife, would that get me into heaven?"

Again, they all answered, "No!"

"Well," I continued, "then how can I get into heaven?"

A five-year-old boy shouted out, "You gotta be dead!"

The answer the Sunday school teacher was looking for was this: Heaven is a gift that must be received. Jesus put it like this: "For God loved this world so much that He gave His only Son, so that anyone who believes in Him will not perish but have eternal life. God didn't send His Son into the world to condemn it, but to save it." (JOHN 3:16–17) These words couldn't be clearer. Jesus didn't come to condemn us—He came to save us. That's the Good News! Eternal life is a gift, but it must be received.

Perhaps this story will help. Two baseball teams were deadlocked in a championship game. It was the bottom of the ninth, two out. The batter hit a shot that ricocheted off the center field wall. He sped around first, second, and third—then raced for home. With the crowd screaming and the relay throw coming, he slid across home plate just before the catcher could make the tag. The crowd went nuts, and the batter's team sprinted out on the field to celebrate. Then, to the shock of everyone listening, the umpire cried, "You're out." Pandemonium ensued. The crowd began booing. The manager went berserk. When the umpire finally got a word in edgewise, he said: "He's not out because he got tagged at home. He's out because he missed first base!"

Establishing a relationship with God is like touching first base. It couldn't be more important. I can attend church, serve on a dozen committees, own the biggest Bible on the block, and memorize the 10 Commandments, but, without a relationship with Christ, someday I will be called out at home.

This isn't about religion. God doesn't care if you're Catholic, Baptist, or Presbyterian or have no religious background. God is interested in having a relationship. He wants you to know His son, Jesus Christ.

Have you ever touched first base? Have you ever said yes to Jesus Christ? Have you told God that you want to know Him; that you want to be part of His family? All you need to do is tell God that you need Him, that you need His forgiveness, His power, and His presence in your life. Why not take that first step by praying the Easter prayer on the following page?

# *An Easter Prayer*

*Dear God, thank You for sending Your Son,*
*Jesus Christ, to earth.*

*I believe Jesus was who He said He was and*
*proved it by rising from death.*

*I want to get to know You personally.*

*Thank You, Jesus, for dying for me and*
*forgiving all my sins.*

*Please forgive me for all my sins and come*
*into my life.*

*I receive You as my Lord and Savior.*

*Thank You for Your free gift of eternal life.*

*Amen.*

*Because of the Resurrection...* **3**

# YOU CAN OVERCOME THE ODDS

*"I am still confident of this: I will see the goodness
of the Lord in the land of the living."*
PSALM 27:13

O N JULY 18, 1929, boxer James J. Braddock stepped into the ring at Yankee Stadium for the biggest fight of his life. Just 24, Braddock had already won close to 40 professional bouts. Now, he was fighting for the light heavyweight championship of the world. But for the first time in his career, Braddock was completely outmatched. He lost in 15 rounds, and the fight was never even close. Tommy Loughran, the reigning champion, made him look helpless.

Braddock lost more than a boxing match that night. His confidence was shot. To make matters worse, the stock market crashed, and he lost everything. Then he broke his hand. He kept boxing, which was the only way to put food on his family's table during the Great Depression. But, he lost 20 times over his next 30 fights. His boxing license was suspended, and he had to go on relief and accept government charity to feed his children.

Then, in 1934, he got a lucky break, when he was a last-minute substitute in a match against "Corn" Griffin, an up-and-coming heavyweight. To everyone's surprise, even his own, Braddock knocked Griffin out. After years of hard luck, Braddock had his confidence back. As portrayed in the film, *Cinderella Man,* Braddock would eventually become heavyweight champion of the world, defeating Max Baer despite being a 10-to-1 underdog. As James Braddock demonstrated, there is no substitute for confidence.

The first words Jesus spoke to the disciples after the Resurrection were these: "Fear not." Because of the Resurrection, we can live with confidence. Nothing else will raise your expectations, give hope, and restore relationships like having confident faith in Jesus Christ.

Notice the impact of faith:

- **Faith in God's PROMISES gives me HOPE!**
  *"Do not be anxious about anything, but in everything, by prayer and petition, with thanksgiving, present your requests to God. And the peace of God, which transcends all understanding, will guard your hearts and your minds in Christ Jesus."* (PHILIPPIANS 4:6–7)

- **Faith in God's CALL gives me PURPOSE!**
  *"For we are God's workmanship, created in Christ Jesus to do good works, which God prepared in advance for us to do."* (EPHESIANS 2:10)

- **Faith in God's WORD gives me DIRECTION!**
  *"All Scripture is God-breathed and is useful for teaching, rebuking, correcting and training in righteousness, so that the man of God may be thoroughly equipped for every good work."* (2 TIMOTHY 3:16–17)

- **Faith in God's POWER gives me CONFIDENCE!**
  *"For I am confident of this very thing, that He who began a good work in you will perfect it until the day of Christ Jesus."* (PHILIPPIANS 1:6)

Gallup once did a poll to study the impact confidence has on people. "If nothing else was different in your life except for one thing, you were confident," Gallup asked, "how different would your life be?" The results: People with a high level of confidence are more satisfied, more willing to help others in need, physically healthier, more productive, and less affected by stress than people with low confidence. They are also more likely to see God as loving, caring, and forgiving.

We can be confident in this, Psalm 27 tells us. We will see "the goodness of the Lord in the land of the living."

*Because of the Resurrection...* **4**

# YOU CAN DISCOVER THAT YOU MATTER TO GOD

*"For God so loved the world that He gave His
one and only Son, that whoever believes in Him
shall not perish but have eternal life."*
JOHN 3:16

*"Jesus said to her, 'Mary.'"*
JOHN 20:16

UTTER DESPAIR AND HOPELESSNESS. That's the picture of Mary on Easter Sunday. Her whole world had crumbled when Jesus was killed. She came to the tomb that day to follow Jewish customs by anointing Jesus' body with spices. At least she could pay her last respects to Him.

When she got to the tomb, Jesus' body was gone. So she stood outside the tomb and wept.

She was so despondent, she didn't recognize Jesus standing beside her. She thought He was the gardener.

"Sir," she said, "if you have carried Him away, tell me where you have put Him, and I will get Him." (JOHN 20:15)

Jesus said one word to her, a word that broke through all the discouragement. One word that lifted her spirit, turned her sorrow to joy, and changed forever the trajectory of her life. One simple word: "Mary." The minute she heard Jesus say her name, Mary realized He was alive. And He knew her name.

That is the message of Easter to people down through the ages. Jesus Christ is alive, and He knows your name. You matter to God more than you will ever know. He created you. He watched you being formed in your mother's womb. He watched you take your first breath. God knows every heartache, every hurt, and every failure you have experienced. And He loves you so much that He came to earth 2,000 years ago and gave His life for you.

Dave Roever knows the power of that kind of relentless, unconditional love. While serving in Vietnam, he suffered burns over 90% of his body when a phosphorus grenade went off next to him. The burns left him horribly disfigured and put him in the hospital for 14 months. He was sent home and treated in a burn unit in a U.S. hospital. One day, the doctors told him that his wife, Brenda, was coming to see him. It would be the first time she'd see how awful he looked.

Later that day, he heard footsteps coming down the hall. But it wasn't Brenda. It was the wife of the man in the next bed. Dave heard her gasp with horror at her husband's condition. Then he watched as she slipped off her wedding ring, gave it back to her husband, and ran from the room. Her final words, "I can't stay with a—a freak," echoed in Dave's ears. Within two weeks, her husband was dead.

Dave steeled himself for his own wife's inevitable reaction. Again, he heard footsteps down the hall. This time, Brenda appeared at the door. Dave watched her eyes as she slowly approached, scanning him from head to toe. Without a word, she bent over and kissed the spot where his lips should have been.

Then, with a smile, she said, "Frankly, in some ways this is an improvement."

"I love you," Brenda told him. "I will always love you. Now let's get you out of here."

Today, the risen Jesus speaks those words to you.

"I love you. I will always love you. I know your name. I will never let you go."

*Because of the Resurrection...* **5**

# YOU CAN EXPERIENCE COMPLETE TRANSFORMATION

*"All I want is to know Christ and to experience
the power of His Resurrection."*
PHILIPPIANS 3:10

JOHN AND MONICA KUBENA WERE IN DIRE STRAITS. A combination of financial difficulties and health problems with their twin daughters, Tara and Sara, who had leukemia, had brought the Kubenas to their knees. The girls had been treated and gone into remission, only to have Tara's leukemia return. A bone marrow transplant helped, but the Kubenas' cramped home was no place for a sick child. Even the slightest infection could be fatal for Tara, so she had to be separated from the rest of the family. The house was too old and too small to keep her safe.

Hope came in the form of hundreds of volunteers from ABC's *Extreme Makeover: Home Edition* television show. The Kubenas' small home was torn down, and a new one, with all the space they needed, was built in a week. Their family was saved. It was, as the show's producer put it, a modern-day fairy tale.

Every week, millions of people tune in to *Extreme Makeover: Home Edition.* The show's producer, Tom Forman, explains why. "It's a guaranteed happy ending," he said in an interview. "There's just something very appealing about saying good things are going to happen to people who desperately need it and deserve it."

The families on the show experience total transformation—from pain and struggle to hope and joy, all in one week's time.

Easter promises transformation. The same power that raised Christ from the dead was unleashed in the lives of His followers and changed them forever. The Apostle John describes the transformation that took place because Jesus rose from the dead. In John 20, the disciples started out confused, and filled with fear. By the end of the chapter, when they saw Jesus alive again, they were filled with hope and peace.

Peter is the best example of this. When Jesus was arrested, all the other disciples ran for their lives. Not Peter. He followed the crowd that arrested Jesus; he wanted to know what happened to Him. Then a servant girl noticed him and accused him of being a friend of Jesus. Others chimed in, recognizing Peter as a disciple. "I never knew Him," Peter said, before running off in shame. However, after the Resurrection, Peter, who was afraid to admit he followed Jesus even to a lowly servant, stood before a huge crowd in Jerusalem and declared the story of the Resurrection. Thousands decided to follow Jesus as a result of Peter's message. Talk about transformation!

The big question is: How can we be transformed by the power of Easter? Where do we find the strength to live like the disciples did? According to the Apostle Paul, another early Christian whose life was turned upside down by the Resurrection, the key to transformation is changing the way you think: "Do not conform any longer to the pattern of this world," he wrote, "but be transformed by the renewing of your mind." (ROMANS 12:2)

One of my mentors, John Maxwell, says that transformation comes in five stages:

1    **When you change your thinking, you change your beliefs.**

2    **When you change your beliefs, you change your expectations.**

3 **When you change your expectations, you change your attitude.**

4 **When you change your attitude, you change your behavior.**

5 **When you change your behavior, you change your life!**

Need an extreme makeover? It all starts here!

*Because of the Resurrection...*

# 6

# YOU CAN LIVE WITH GOD'S POWER

*"Those who wait on the Lord will renew their strength.*
*They will soar on wings like eagles; they will run and*
*not grow weary, they will walk and not be faint."*
ISAIAH 40:31

IF YOU'RE EVER UP LATE AT NIGHT, clicking through channels looking for something to watch, you may have come across the World's Strongest Man Competition. These 300-pound guys do all kinds of incredible things, like tearing phonebooks in half, carrying 250-pound rocks, and eating Volkswagens—trying to prove they're the world's strongest men.

That kind of strength is impressive, but none of them could match the power that Jesus demonstrated. People flocked to Him because they saw Him heal with a touch. They saw blind people who could see again, paralyzed people who could walk again, and lepers who were cleansed. Once, He even spoke to the wind and waves in the middle of a raging storm, and the storm disappeared.

When Jesus stretched out His arms and hung on the cross, the crowds that watched Him die thought they were seeing weakness. They were wrong. They were seeing the power of God like it had never been displayed before. Then, on Easter Sunday, Jesus walked out of the grave, conquering even death itself. And He offers that same power to each of us today.

The power that defeated death can give you the power to live life. If God can raise Jesus from the dead, He can raise a dead marriage. He can raise a dead career. He can raise a dead dream. He can give you strength to keep going when you feel you can't take another step. And at the end of your life, God will throw His arms around you and welcome you into His presence. That's the power of Easter.

The Bible tells us we can experience the power of the Resurrection, that God can do "immeasurably more than all we ask or imagine, according to His power that is at work within us." (EPHESIANS 3:20) This verse says that the greatest power ever demonstrated on Earth is available to every single person on Earth.

I heard a story recently that shows what it's like to live without that kind of power. A farmer had some trees to clear, so he went out to buy a new chainsaw. A salesman sold him one guaranteed to cut down 15 trees in one day.

A week later, the unhappy farmer brought the saw back to the store and demanded to see the salesman. The farmer wanted his money back; he'd worked all week and only cut down three trees. "You sold me a piece of junk," he told the salesman.

The salesman apologized and asked if he could look at the saw. He pulled the cord, and the chainsaw started right up, with the familiar "Bzzzz" sound.

"Hey," demanded the startled farmer, "what's that noise?"

How many of us are like that farmer, trying to live through our own strength, never knowing the power that we could have, if we would only ask?

*Because of the Resurrection...*

# 7

# YOU CAN TRUST YOUR BIBLE

*"For what I received I passed on to you as of first importance: that Christ died for our sins according to the Scriptures, that He was buried, that He was raised on the third day according to the Scriptures...."*
1 CORINTHIANS 15:3–4

YEARS AGO, I spoke at a large youth convention in California, and a high school sophomore came up to me during a break.

"Dude," he said in typical Valley speak, "You're an awesome speaker."

"Thanks, dude," I responded, "you're an awesome listener."

Then he said, "Dude, there's only one problem. The Bible you're talking about isn't true! It's full of errors and stuff."

"Bummer," I said. "Looks like I'm going to have to get a new job. But before I quit, let me ask you: Which parts of the Bible aren't true?"

"I don't know," he admitted.

"And which errors are you talking about?"

Same answer: "I don't know."

Finally, I asked, "Have you ever read the Bible?"

You can probably guess the answer. "Nope," he said.

Unfortunately, my young friend isn't alone. Many people assume that the Bible isn't accurate or authoritative. They often are unaware about the claims of Christ or about the compelling evidence for trusting the Bible.

A few things you may not know about the Bible:

- **The Bible is unique in its circulation.** It has been read by more people than any other book in human history. Find me another book that's been at the top of the best-seller list for 400 years.

- **The Bible is unique in its translation.** Even though it's been translated into more than 1,200 languages already, a literal army of translators is working today to make it available to still more people.

- **The Bible is unique in its durability.** It has survived bans and burnings, ridicule and criticism. The Bible has outlived every one of its cruelest opponents.

- **The Bible is unique in its impact.** Millions of people credit the Bible for transforming their lives, altering their view of the world, changing their relationships, their values, and their view of eternity.

- **The Bible is unique in its historical reliability.** Josh McDowell, in his book, *Evidence That Demands a Verdict*, points out that "no other ancient document even comes close" to the historical reliability of the New Testament.

In Matthew 16, Jesus makes a remarkable promise. He tells His disciples that He is going to be arrested, beaten, and killed by the authorities in Jerusalem. Then, "on the third day," He would rise from the grave. All the other promises that Jesus made in Scripture, that our sins will be forgiven, that God will provide for us, that Jesus is with us always, all depend upon the Resurrection. If Christ was raised, we can trust the Bible's promises.

The Apostle Paul lays it on the line in 1 Corinthians 15: "If Christ has not been raised, our preaching is useless and so is your faith."

But Christ has been raised, Paul declares. Because of that fact, we can trust in the promises of the Bible.

Voltaire, the noted French skeptic who died in 1778, said that in one hundred years from his time, Christianity would be swept from existence and pass into history. Fifty years after his death, the Geneva Bible Society used his press and began printing Bibles in his house.

Skeptics come and go, but the Bible survives. Bernard Ramm said, "The death knell has sounded a hundred times for the Bible, but the corpse never stays put."

*Because of the Resurrection...*

# 8

# YOU CAN LIVE WITH GOD'S JOY

*"May the God of hope fill you with all joy*
*and peace as you trust in Him...."*
ROMANS 15:13

MARTIN LUTHER WAS IN A RUT. For days, he sulked around the house, lost in depression. Finally, his wife had enough. One morning, she came downstairs dressed in black and ready for a funeral.

"Who died?" Luther asked.

"God," she replied.

Luther rebuked her, saying, "What do you mean, God is dead? God cannot die."

"Well, the way you've been acting I was sure He had!"

I love the Brennan Manning line, "If you have the joy of the Lord in your heart, please notify your face." Too many Christians look like poster children for the book of Lamentations—ask how they're doing, and the vinegar-for-lunch-bunch answers, "Pretty good, under the circumstances." I am tempted to ask: "What are you doing there?"

During some of his darkest days, the Apostle Paul wrote the most positive book in the Bible, the New Testament book of Philippians. Again and again, in this four-chapter manual on joy, Paul told us to "rejoice" and "be joyful."

The remarkable thing about Philippians is this: Paul wrote it while he was in prison, literally in chains for preaching about Jesus.

This life-changing letter gives us four Joy Builders:

- **God finishes what He starts: TRUST HIM!**
  *"Being confident of this, that He who began a good work in you will carry it on to completion until the day of Christ Jesus."* (PHILIPPIANS 1:6)

- **God's forgiveness is complete: BELIEVE HIM!**
  *"Forgetting what is behind and straining toward what is ahead, I press on toward the goal to win the prize for which God has called me heavenward in Christ Jesus."* (PHILIPPIANS 3:13–14)

- **Worry is destructive: RELEASE IT!**
  *"Do not be anxious about anything, but in everything, by prayer and petition, with thanksgiving, present your requests to God."* (PHILIPPIANS 4:6)

- **Gratitude is healthy: EXPRESS IT!**
  *"I thank my God every time I remember you. In all my prayers for all of you, I always pray with joy...."* (PHILIPPIANS 1:3–5)

Joy is essential to healthy living, but it's not automatic! A lack of joy ought to be like a warning light on the dashboard of your life. It's a sure sign you need to go back to one of the four Joy Builders.

*Because of the Resurrection...*  9

# YOU CAN LIVE WITH A SENSE OF WONDER

*"When He had led them out to the vicinity of Bethany, He lifted up His hands and blessed them. While He was blessing them, He left them and was taken up into heaven. Then they worshiped Him and returned to Jerusalem with great joy. And they stayed continually at the temple, praising God."*

LUKE 24:49–53

ONE OF MY FAVORITE AUTHORS is Robert Fulghum, author of books like *All I Really Needed to Know I Learned in Kindergarten.* (Unfortunately, I read that one after spending $30,000 on graduate school!) In his book *Uh-Oh,* he asks an interesting question: Why are five-year-olds so much more creative than college students?

Here's what Fulghum writes:

"Ask a kindergarten class, How many of you can draw? And all hands shoot up. Yes, of course we can draw, all of us. What can you draw? Anything! How about a dog eating a fire truck in a jungle? Sure! How big you want it? How many of you can sing? All hands. Of course we sing! What can you sing? Anything! What if you don't know the words? No problem, we make them up."

He goes on to ask if five-year-olds can dance, play musical instruments, write poems, act in plays, or do almost anything creative. The answer is always the same. Yes, we can! "The children are confident in spirit, infinite in resources, and eager to learn," he says. "Everything is still possible."

But ask those same questions of college kids, and you'll get a whole different answer. Almost everyone will say no. Even those who say yes are tentative: "I only play piano, I only draw horses, I only dance to rock and roll, I only sing in the shower."

Then Fulghum asks a crucial question: What went wrong? What happened to stomp out the God-given creativity and zest for living? What happened to the enthusiasm that God put into the heart of every child?

The answer is simple. We have forgotten how awesome life is. Instead, we settle for humdrum existence, plodding along from day to day. We settle for routine instead of romance. We settle for low-level living instead of following our dream. We don't risk much. We don't celebrate much. And, sadly, we don't laugh much. That may be why it is so rare to find a teenager who is excited about becoming an adult. Who in their right mind really wants to lose their sense of wonder?

So how do we regain that sense of wonder? We remember who we are. We remember that we are God's children, and we have an incredible Father.

Diane Disney tells the story of the day she found out who her father was. Walt Disney and his wife were not normal Hollywood parents. Instead of seeking the spotlight, they tried to shield their two daughters from publicity. They wanted their girls to have a normal childhood.

Every day, Walt drove his kids to their public school. He took them to swim class and dance lessons. He arranged his schedule so that he could take them just like any normal father.

Diane Disney remembers that she didn't even know what her daddy did for a living.

To her, he was just "Dad."

One day, a friend at school asked her: "What's it like having Walt Disney as your dad?"

Later that day, Diane found her dad sitting in his favorite chair. She stood next to him, outraged. "You never told me you were Walt

Disney!" she said.

Diane couldn't believe it. She knew Walt Disney. Walt Disney was her dad. For a week, she wandered in a daze. Every time she saw a cartoon or watched the *Mickey Mouse Club*, she thought, "Walt Disney is my dad."

That's the sense of wonder God wants for us. Forget Walt Disney. The same God who made the universe, who raised Jesus from dead, is our Dad. That staggering realization should fill us with awe.

The message of Easter is this: God wins. Love triumphs. Death is defeated forever.

And God, our Dad, did it.

*Because of the Resurrection...*

# 10

# You Can Trust His Claims

*"Jesus said, 'I am the Son of God. Don't believe*
*Me unless I do miracles of God.'"*
John 10:36-37

JESUS CHRIST MADE OUTRAGEOUS CLAIMS. He claimed to be able to forgive sin (MARK 2:10). He claimed to be the Way, the Truth, and the Life (JOHN 14:6). He predicted that He would be killed but then would rise from the dead (MATTHEW 16:21). He even claimed to be the Son of God (JOHN 10:36–37).

The Resurrection claim of Jesus Christ separates Him from every other religious leader. No one else, not Buddha, Mohammed, Joseph Smith (founder of Mormonism), or Mary Baker Eddy (founder of Christian Science), made such outrageous claims. No one else in history has come back from the dead to prove their claims were true.

However, Thomas didn't believe it when the other disciples told him that Jesus had risen from the dead. "Unless I see the nail marks in His hands and put my finger where the nails were, and put my hand into His side," Thomas told them, "I will not believe it." (JOHN 20:25)

A week later, Jesus appeared and stood next to Thomas. He looked at Thomas and said: "Put your finger here; see My hands. Reach out your hand and put it into My side. Stop doubting and believe." (JOHN 20:27)

From that moment on, Thomas was a changed man. He left that room in Jerusalem, where he saw Jesus, and carried the message of the Resurrection far and wide. He traveled to Babylon (now Iraq) and Persia (now Iran) and may have traveled as far as India telling people everywhere he went about the death and Resurrection of Jesus.

What does the Resurrection mean? It means that:

- **Jesus is who He claimed to be.**
  *"I am the Resurrection and the Life. He who believes in Me will live, even though he dies."* (JOHN 11:25)

- **Jesus has the power He claimed to have.**
  *"All power in Heaven and on earth is given to Me."* (MATTHEW 28:18)

- **Jesus keeps His promises.**
  *"I will be with you always."* (MATTHEW 28:20)

What does the Resurrection mean? It means you can relax because you can trust His claims!

*Because of the Resurrection...*

# 11

# YOU CAN LIVE WITH GOD'S PURPOSE

*"David served God's purpose in his generation...."*
ACTS 13:36

I LOVE LIVING AND BEING A PASTOR in Granite Bay, CA. The town has it all: beautiful lake, great people, wonderful weather, excellent schools; all in all, an idyllic American suburb. However, many people in our community have a lot to live on, and too little to live for. They have an abundance of possessions but a scarcity of purpose. And without purpose, all the possessions and possibilities are worthless.

Our culture is starving for purpose. Over the past few years, Rick Warren's book, *The Purpose-Driven Life,* has sold more than 20 million copies, a sure sign that millions of people are looking for meaning in life. They want something bigger to live for.

Without purpose, these three things happen:

- **Life loses passion:** Ralph Barton, one of the top cartoonists in the nation, left this note pinned to his pillow before taking his own life: "I have had few difficulties, many friends, great successes; I have gone from wife to wife, from house to house, visited great countries of the world, but I am fed up with inventing devices to fill up 24 hours of the day."

- **Life loses meaning:** "A myriad of men are born; they labor and sweat and struggle ... they squabble and scold and fight; they scramble for little mean advantages over each other; age creeps upon them; infirmities follow; ... those they love are taken from them, and the joy of life is turned to aching grief. It (the release) comes at last—the only unpoisoned gift earth ever had for them—and they vanish from a world where they were of no consequence, a world which will lament them a day and forget them forever."
—MARK TWAIN (shortly before his death)

- **Life loses joy and significance:** "This is the true joy in life, the being used for a purpose recognized by yourself as a mighty one: the being thoroughly worn out before you are thrown on the scrap heap, and being a force of nature instead of a feverish selfish little clod of ailments and grievances, complaining that the world will not devote itself to making you happy."
—GEORGE BERNARD SHAW

When I was a youth pastor years ago, I took a group of teenagers from a wealthy community on a mission trip. At first, the students were disappointed. It was Sunday morning, and we had just arrived at the church in Mexico that was to serve as our headquarters for a week of ministry. The students had spent three months planning, preparing, and praying that God would use them on this trip. But something had gone wrong. The church where we were going to serve had been badly burned; the roof had caved in, and now only the four walls remained.

We arrived as the pastor was midway through the Sunday service. We filed into the back of the burned-out church, greeted only by the amazed stares of the nine parishioners. After a few minutes, the pastor stopped the service and asked what we were doing there.

It turned out that he had no idea we were coming. The mission board we worked with had neglected to inform him. There was a long silence until one of the student leaders explained that we were Christians and were there to serve.

I will never forget what followed. The pastor, choking back tears, told us that some villagers had burned the church down six months earlier. "We've been praying that God would send help," he said, "but had given up hope of help ever coming!"

Our kids were stunned. Although they had heard a million times that God desired to use their lives, they were now experiencing it for the first time.

During a team meeting later, one student said in amazement, "We are an answer to prayer!" He was right on target. Back home, these students were viewed by others, and occasionally themselves, as problems. But when we gave them a purpose, to go out and serve in love, they became an answer to someone's prayer.

God asks something great of every one of us. He made you, gave you gifts and talents, and put you right where you are, not so that you could live for yourself, but so that you could be the answer to someone's prayers.

*Because of the Resurrection...* **12**

# YOU CAN KNOW GOD

*"Your word is a lamp to my feet and a light for my path."*
PSALM 119:105

*"I am the Light of the World."*
JOHN 8:12

A LITTLE BOY sat down at the kitchen table with his crayons and a big sheet of blank paper, and he started to draw. His father, noticing his son hard at work at the table, stopped to look.

"What are you doing?" he asked.

"I'm drawing a picture of God," the little boy said.

"But, son," the father said, "you can't draw a picture of God. Nobody knows what God looks like."

The little boy thought for a moment and said, "Well—they will when I get through!"

There are a lot of false, sometimes bizarre, ideas about God out in the world. Most of them sound like they were made up out of thin air, much like the picture drawn by that little boy. The other day I typed "God" into a Yahoo search. It came back with 43 million hits.

Times haven't changed. Back in 1947, C.S. Lewis told *Time* magazine that he knew of a student whose parents said that she should think of God as "pure substance." The problem, she told Lewis, was that she ended up thinking of God as a "vast tapioca pudding." "To make matters worse," Lewis said, "she disliked tapioca."

Other people think of God as an angry judge who sits on His throne, just waiting for us to do something wrong so He can zap us from on high. No wonder people avoid God—run from God, fear God, and avoid church like the plague. There are all these misconceptions of what He is like—"This is the day the Lord has made," has turned into: "This is the Lord that the day has made." The problem with all this is that it's possible to be sincere but sincerely wrong. We need an authoritative word from one with the credibility of rising from the dead.

Jesus showed us a very different view of God. He shattered the myths built up about God. While many people believe God is distant and detached, the Bible calls Jesus "Emmanuel," which means "God with us." Instead of an uncaring cosmic force, Jesus showed us a God who knows every detail of our lives: "Every hair on your head is numbered," Jesus told His followers. (MATTHEW 10:30)

Having a clear view of God puts the world in proper perspective. Like turning on a light in a dark room, it helps us see things as they really are.

A mom named Leslie Johnston knows how important that can be. One night, her kids were complaining about all the mosquitoes. Rather than turning on the light, and risk having the kids wide awake for the rest of the night, she decided to go into their room and spray insect repellent in the dark. When she was done, she went to bed.

The next morning she discovered, to her horror, that she had covered the bedding, the walls of their room, and the kids with blue spray paint. "I thought it smelled kind of funny," she said later.

Life doesn't work well when you can't see clearly! If you don't know Jesus Christ, you're in the dark. You're just kind of stumbling along through life, unable to see God or understand your purpose in life. You don't really see clearly unless you know the "Light of the World."

Do you want to get to know God? It's simple. Get to know Jesus Christ. Jesus said, "Anyone who has seen Me has seen the Father." (JOHN 14:9)

*Because of the Resurrection...*

# 13

# YOU CAN LIVE WITH GOD'S GUIDANCE AND DIRECTION

*"Do not conform any longer to the pattern of this world, but be transformed by the renewing of your mind. Then you will be able to test and approve what God's will is—His good, pleasing and perfect will."*
ROMANS 12:2

I LOVE a story penned by the eminent theologian Dr. Seuss:

*"The Zode"*

*Did I ever tell you about the young Zode?*
*Who came to two signs at the fork in the road?*
*One said Place one, and the other, Place two.*
*So the Zode had to make up his mind what to do.*
*Well ... the Zode scratched his head, and his chin and his pants.*
*And he said to himself, "I'll be taking a chance*
*If I go to Place one. Now, that place may be hot!*
*And so, how do I know if I'll like it or not?*
*On the other hand though, I'll be sort of a fool*
*If I go to Place two and I find it too cool,*
*In that case I may catch a chill and turn blue!*
*So, maybe Place one is the best, not Place two*
*But then again, what if Place one is too high?*

*I may catch a terrible earache and die!*
*So Place two may be best! On the other hand though...*
*What might happen to me if Place two is too low?*
*I might get some very strange pain in my toe!*
*So Place one may be best." And he started to go.*
*Then he stopped and he said, "On the other hand though...*
*On the other hand...other hand...other hand though...."*
*And for 36 hours and a half that poor Zode*
*Made starts and made stops at the fork in the road.*
*Saying, "Don't take a chance. No! You may not be right."*
*Then he got an idea that was wonderfully bright!*
*"Play safe!" cried the Zode. "I'll play safe! I'm no dunce!*
*I'll simply start out for both places at once!"*
*And that's how the Zode who would not take a chance*
*Got to no place at all with a split in his pants.*

A lot of us are like that Zode: getting nowhere spiritually because we can't make a decision, like the man who went to see a psychiatrist for advice because he was having trouble making up his mind.

"Are you indecisive?" the psychiatrist asked him.

"Yes and no," the man said.

"What do you mean by that?" the doctor said.

"Well, I used to be indecisive, but now I'm not sure."

Talk about paralysis by analysis. These days, people try all kinds of systems looking for guidance from God: astrology, numerology, metaphysical books, even psychic hotlines.

As we pursue God's best for our lives, two principles can help cut through the fog:

- **God's will is found in God's word, the Bible.** As we read His word, God speaks to us. If we ignore God's word, we ignore God. The motto of Detroit Bible College best summarizes this principle: "Discovering the will of God by studying the word of God." Through the principles, commands, and examples of Scripture, we discover His will.

- **God's will never contradicts God's word.** People will often tell me that they "feel" God is leading them in a certain direction. My first reaction is always the same: "What does the Bible say about it?" We can save a lot of confusion by asking that one simple question. The Apostle Paul tells us that if we conform our minds to God's word, we will know God's will.

Our destinies are determined not by chance, but by the choices we make. Choose wisely. Find God's will for your life in God's word.

*Because of the Resurrection...*    **14**

# YOU CAN LIVE WITH PASSION

*"Never be lacking in zeal, but keep your spiritual fervor."*
ROMANS 12:11

A N EXHAUSTED PERSON WROTE THE FOLLOWING:
*Yes, I'm tired. For several years I've been blaming it on middle age, iron-poor blood, lack of vitamins, air pollution, water pollution, saccharin, obesity, dieting, underarm odor, yellow wax build-up, and a dozen other maladies that make you wonder if life is really worth living.*

*But now I find out that I'm tired because I'm overworked.*

*The population of this country is 200 million. Eighty-four million are retired. That leaves 116 million to do the work. There are 75 million in school, which leaves 41 million to do the work. Of this total, there are 22 million employed by the federal government.*

*That leaves 19 million to do the work. Four million are in the armed forces, which leaves 15 million to do the work. Take from that total the 14,800,000 people who work for the state and city governments and that leaves 200,000 to do the work. There are 188,000 in hospitals, so that leaves 12,000 to do the work. Now, there are 11,998 people in prisons.*

*That leaves just two people to do the work. You and me. And you're sitting there reading this. No wonder I'm tired.*

Many of us can relate to that statement. We're worn out. We're living at a hamster's pace, racing faster and faster, getting nowhere and losing our passion for God and life in the process. Paul warned about this condition when he said, "Never be lacking in zeal, but keep your spiritual fervor." (ROMANS 12:11) The key word is "keep." That means it's not automatic; you don't stay on fire for God automatically. You can lose your enthusiasm for God and start going through the motions.

The disciples felt like that. When Jesus died, they lost their zeal for living and faced a future without hope or purpose. When Jesus came back from the grave, the disciples were reborn. They were ready to live out Jesus' commandment. Feel the passion in this verse: "Love the Lord your God with all your heart and with all your soul and with all your mind and with all your strength and love your neighbor as yourself." (MARK 12:30–31)

God doesn't want us to live life in a half-hearted way. He wants whole-hearted passion, the kind of passion that can make a difference.

Some years ago, Chuck Colson befriended Jack Eckerd, founder of the Eckerd Drug stores. Together, they traveled on Jack Eckerd's Lear jet advocating criminal justice reforms, and everywhere they went Jack Eckerd would introduce Chuck Colson to the crowds and say, "This is Chuck Colson, my friend; I met him on Bill Buckley's television program. He's born again, I'm not. I wish I were."

After many conversations with Colson, and after reading *Mere Christianity*, Eckerd finally accepted that Jesus was resurrected from the dead and he decided to follow Him.

Soon afterward, Eckerd went into one of his stores, and walked by the magazine rack, where he saw *Playboy* and *Penthouse.* He'd seen them there many times before, but it had never bothered him. Now he saw them with new eyes and wanted them out of his stores.

When Eckerd told his management about his decision, they protested. "You can't mean that, Mr. Eckerd," one executive said. "We make $3 million a year on those books."

Eckerd said simply, "Take 'em out of my stores." Later, Colson asked him, "Did you do that because of your commitment to Christ?" Eckerd replied, "Why else would I give away $3 million? The Lord wouldn't let me off the hook."

The ripple effect of Eckerd's decision was dramatic. In the next 12 months, 11,000 retail outlets in America removed *Playboy* and *Penthouse*, not because somebody passed a law but because God wouldn't let one of his men off the hook.

That's the kind of passion that brings change.

*Because of the Resurrection...*

# 15

# YOU CAN OVERCOME DISCOURAGEMENT

*"The Lord Himself goes before you and will be*
*with you; He will never leave you nor forsake you.*
*Do not be afraid; do not be discouraged."*
DEUTERONOMY 31:7–9

AS A FATHER OF FOUR, I love the following story:

*Four expectant fathers were in a hospital waiting room while their wives were in labor. The nurse arrived and announced to the first man, "Congratulations, sir! You're the father of twins." "What a coincidence!" the man said. "I work for the Minnesota Twins baseball team."*

*A little while later, the nurse returned with news for the second man: "You, sir, are the father of triplets." "Wow! That's an incredible coincidence," he responded. "I work for 3M."*

*An hour later, the nurse came back. This time she turned to the third man, who had been very quiet in the corner. His wife, she said, had just given birth to quadruplets. He responded with stunned silence. "Don't tell me, another coincidence?" the nurse asked. "I don't believe it," he said after regaining his composure. "I work for the Four Seasons Hotel."*

*At this, the fourth man let out a scream and fainted dead away. The nurse rushed to his side. When he regained consciousness, he mumbled the same phrase over and over again: "Why did I take that job at 7-Eleven?"*

Ever felt like that? Life can suddenly get overwhelming. Hope can quickly turn to discouragement. Rick Warren says that discouragement is:

- **A universal disease**— we all get it.

- **A contagious disease**— you can catch it from those around you.

- **A repeating disease**— you can catch it more than once.

- **A deadly disease**— discouragement can wreck your life and ruin your relationships.

As a pastor, I have seen more people walk away from God, marriage, and effective living because of discouragement than any other factor. That's why at Bayside we constantly give people the following definition of discouragement: "Discouragement is the anesthetic that the devil uses on a person just before he reaches in and carves out their heart."

The root problem with discouragement is this: People give up! On God. On their marriage. On their kids. On their church. On their ministry. On life itself.

Discouraged? Maybe the following parable will help:

A farmer owned an old mule. The mule fell into the farmer's well. The farmer heard the mule braying or whatever mules do when they fall into wells. After assessing the situation, the farmer sympathized with the mule but decided that neither the mule nor the well was worth the trouble of saving. Instead, he called his neighbors together and told them what had happened and enlisted their help to haul dirt to bury the old mule in the well and put him out of his misery.

Initially, the old mule was hysterical. But as the farmer and his neighbors continued shoveling and the dirt hit the mule's back, a thought struck him. Every time a shovel load of dirt landed on his back he should shake it off and step up! This he did, blow after blow.

"Shake it off and step up—shake it off and step up!" he repeated to encourage himself. No matter how painful the blows, or distressing the situation seemed, the old mule fought panic and just kept right on shaking it off and stepping up. It wasn't long before the old mule, battered and exhausted, stepped triumphantly over the wall of that well.

What seemed like it would bury him actually blessed him...all because of the manner in which he handled his adversity. That's life! If we refuse to give in to discouragement and self pity, the adversities that come along to bury us usually have, within them, the potential to benefit and bless us!

Now, back up 2,000 years. It's the first Easter, and everything has gone wrong. On Palm Sunday, Jesus is practically crowned king. Five days later, He's dead, and the disciples are hunted criminals.

On Easter Sunday, when they saw Jesus alive, their hope and confidence were restored. Two of the disciples described their encounter with Jesus this way: "Were not our hearts burning within us while He talked with us on the road and opened the Scriptures to us?" (LUKE 24:32)

God wants to set our hearts on fire, so we can serve Him with confidence and joy.

The prophet Isaiah told us that God gives strength to the weary and increases the power of the weak.

"Even youths grow tired and weary, and young men stumble and fall," Isaiah said, "but those who hope in the Lord will renew their strength. They will soar on wings like eagles; they will run and not grow weary; they will walk and not be faint." (ISAIAH 40:29–31)

*Because of the Resurrection...*

# 16

# YOU CAN
# OVERCOME FEAR

*"I prayed to the Lord, and He answered
me; He freed me from all my fears."*
PSALM 34:4

IT'S EMBARRASSING TO ADMIT IT, but I'm a recovering coward. Twelve short years ago, I was having a great time not being a pastor. I was speaking, writing, and in general having a blast. Then my wife, Carol, and I were invited to start a new church in Granite Bay, CA. I immediately applied this verse: "Lord, here am I, send someone else," and turned the invitation down.

Truth be told, I was afraid. Afraid of failing. Afraid no one would show up. Afraid of having to raise money. Afraid that, because the new church was in California, we would get sued in the process (that happened, by the way).

Plus, I was a dad with four young kids. Dads with four young kids don't start churches. It's way too risky.

I then made the mistake of attending a three-day prayer summit with 800 Christian leaders from around the world. Three hours into a late-night prayer meeting, I had prayed for everything I could think of—twice! Then, this idea occurred to me: I should pray for Bayside, the new church, that God would give them the right pastor, because it sure wasn't going to be me!

While I was praying, I heard God speak to me. The message was crystal clear: "Read Acts 18." I opened my Bible and read the following:

"Do not be afraid; keep on speaking; do not be silent. For I am with you, and no one is going to attack and harm you, because I have many people in this city." (ACTS 18:19) I believe God said to me, if you accept this invitation to plant a church, I will rally people to help you.

I still didn't want to plant the church. So I decided to keep reading, looking for a loophole. I didn't find one. Instead, the next verse said, "Paul stayed for a year and a half, teaching them the word of God."

I walked out of the prayer meeting and called my wife (you husbands will understand this), to find out if I'd really heard from God. Carol said she'd felt God calling us to start this church and was wondering when I'd figure it out. The rest is history.

Bayside has been the best thing that has happened in all my years of ministry. The church exploded out of the gate. Thousands of people have come to Christ, including some relatives whom we had spent more than 20 years praying for. These have been the best 12 years of my life, and I almost missed them for one reason: **FEAR**.

The problem with fear is this: Fear paralyzes. Fear is a self-imposed prison where confidence and hope are locked out, and fear and anxiety are locked in. Fear will keep you from discovering God's vision for your life and from experiencing the best years of your life.

Remember this:

- The first words the angels spoke after Jesus Christ rose from the dead were: **"Don't be afraid."**

- The first words the disciples heard after Jesus Christ rose from the dead were: **"Don't be afraid."**

- The first words Jesus spoke to His disciples after He rose from the grave were the same: **"Don't be afraid."**

We have a definition for fear we use at Bayside: "Fear is the dark-room where negativity develops." Is God calling you to start something, serve somewhere, give something, and you're afraid to launch? If so, go for it! You could be on the first day of the best 12-year run of your life!

Jesus Christ is risen from the dead. Don't be afraid.

*Because of the Resurrection...*   **17**

# YOU CAN TRUST HIS PROMISES

*"Jesus did many other miraculous signs in the presence of His disciples, which are not recorded in this book. But these are written that you may believe that Jesus is the Christ, the Son of God, and that by believing you may have life in His name."*
JOHN 20:30–31

IN HIS BOOK, *When All You've Ever Wanted Isn't Enough,* Rabbi Harold Kushner tells the following story:

*I was sitting on a beach one summer day, watching two children, a boy and a girl, playing in the sand. They were hard at work building an elaborate sandcastle by the water's edge, with gates and towers and moats and internal passages. Just when they had nearly finished their project, a big wave came along and knocked it down, reducing it to a heap of wet sand. I expected the children to burst into tears, devastated by what had happened to all their hard work. But they surprised me. Instead, they ran up the shore away from the water, laughing and holding hands, and sat down to build another castle. I realized that they had taught me an important lesson. All the things in our lives, all the complicated structures we spent so much time and energy creating, are built on sand. Sooner or later, the wave will come along and knock down what we have worked so hard to build, and when that happens only the person who has somebody's hand to hold will be able to laugh.*

During the storms of life, we need something firm to hold on to. Nothing lifts my spirit more than holding on to God's promises. God has promises for almost every circumstance. Let me give you some examples:

- **Every time you pick up a Bible,** remember Jesus' promise: *"Heaven and earth will pass away, but My words will never pass away."* (MATTHEW 24:35)

- **Every time you come to worship,** remember Jesus' promise: *"Where two or three have gathered together in My name, I am there in their midst."* (MATTHEW 18:20)

- **Every time you feel alone,** remember Jesus' promise: *"I will be with you always, even to the end of the world."* (MATTHEW 28:20)

- **Every time you feel weak,** remember God's promise: *"The Lord is faithful, and He will strengthen and protect you from the evil one."* (2 THESSALONIANS 3:3)

- **Every time you have failed,** remember God's promise: *"If we confess our sins, He is faithful and just and will forgive us our sins and purify us from all unrighteousness."* (1 JOHN 1:9)

- **Every time you are tempted to lose hope,** remember God's promise: *"Let us hold unswervingly to the hope we profess, for He who promised is faithful."* (HEBREWS 10:23)

- **And when you stand on the brink of death,** remember Jesus' promise: *"In My Father's house are many rooms ... I am going there to prepare a place for you. And if I go and prepare a place for you, I will come back and* *take you to be with Me. For where I am, there you will be also."* (MATTHEW 14:2–4)

One Scripture sums it up: "The Lord's loving kindnesses indeed never cease, for His compassions never fail. They are new every morning; great is Your faithfulness." (LAMENTATIONS 3:22–23)

*Because of the Resurrection...*

# 18

# YOU CAN CHANGE DIRECTION

*"...Neither do I condemn you," Jesus declared.*
*"Go now and leave your life of sin."*
JOHN 8:11

*"Therefore, if anyone is in Christ, he is a new*
*creation; the old has gone; the new has come!"*
2 CORINTHIANS 5:17

THE MOST DISCOURAGING WORDS in the English language are these: "You will never change!" Those four words destroy lives. They steal vitality. They replace clear hope for a better future with the icy fog of confusion and despair.

Jesus never uttered those words! Whenever He came across someone who had failed or had lost hope, He offered them the chance to start again. In John 8, a woman was caught having an affair, and religious leaders dragged her before Jesus, in hopes that He would condemn her. They wanted to stone her. (Interestingly, they let the man she was having an affair with go scot-free.)

Jesus said, "Fine, go ahead. There's just one catch. If any one of you is without sin, let him be the first to throw a stone at her."

Once the crowd had dispersed, leaving behind a large pile of unused stones, Jesus looked at the woman. "Woman, where are they? Has no one condemned you?" He asked.

"No one, sir," she said.

"Then neither do I condemn you," Jesus told her. "Go now and leave your life of sin."

Not only did Jesus show mercy to her; He also invited her to change direction and start again.

One of my favorite stories is told by Earl Palmer. He and several West Coast friends went to seminary on the East Coast. This meant that almost any holiday was an occasion to pile in a car and head home to the West Coast. Wanting to get home as fast as possible, they drove straight through, each taking a three-hour turn behind the wheel while the other guys slept.

During one of their trips home, Earl was driving through Iowa in the middle of the night when he passed a gas station. The car was low on gas, and it was about time to change drivers, so Earl made a U-turn. He went back to the gas station and filled up the tank, then woke the next driver, climbed into the back seat and fell fast asleep.

Since Earl neglected to mention the U-turn, his friend spent three hours driving east as fast as he could, with no idea he was heading in the wrong direction. About six in the morning, the friend began to suspect he was heading the wrong way. He woke Earl up, and his worst fears were realized. Sheepishly, the friend told Earl that he'd ignored several signs that he was headed in the wrong direction: mileage signs, road signs, even a Greyhound bus going by with "Las Vegas" on the destination sign.

"I ignored all those signs until I saw the sunrise in my windshield," he said. "When I saw the sun come up, that was too big a sign to ignore."

The Son of God rising from the grave at Easter is too big a sign to ignore. It should capture our attention and cause us to pull over and rethink the direction of our lives.

The good news is that God allows U-turns, no matter how long we've been driving in the wrong direction.

*Because of the Resurrection...*    **19**

# YOU CAN EXPERIENCE
# GOD'S PRESENCE

*"... And surely I am with you always, to the very end of the age."*
MATTHEW 28:20

NEWLYWED NORA NAGARUK'S PLANS and dreams were coming true. Ever since she was a young girl, growing up in a small village in Alaska, Nora had dreamed of becoming a doctor. By the summer of 2004, she'd completed 11 years of training: four years at the University of Oklahoma, another four at the University of Washington School of Medicine, a year of internship, and two years of residency. One more year of residency, and her lifelong goal of being a doctor would be reality.

Then, just before her first wedding anniversary, she got what she thought was a bad cold. When it didn't go away, she went in for a few tests, convinced that her nagging sore throat and fatigue were due to a case of mononucleosis or perhaps strep throat. In those days, due to the demands of her residency, she was sleeping only a few hours each night. Nora thought the lack of sleep had finally caught up to her.

Tests for mono and strep throat came back negative. Meanwhile, Nora got sicker and sicker. "It was like the life was draining out of me," she said. Finally, a blood test revealed that she had acute myelocytic leukemia—the same cancer that had killed her father, 15 years earlier. A few days later, she was on a flight from her home in Alaska to Seattle to begin cancer treatments.

Faced with this life-threatening illness, Nora and her husband, Nathan, could have been overwhelmed. But from the first days in the hospital, their friends and family surrounded them with love and support. They came and visited, called, emailed, and, most important of all, prayed for Nora.

The illness changed the way Nora saw God. At the worst moments, when all her dreams had been taken away and death seemed just a step away, God was with her.

"You know things about God's character—that He is loving and caring," she said, "but when you are lying in a hospital bed and you can feel people praying for you, it's like God has come down to your bedside."

On the first Easter, the followers of Jesus made amazing discoveries, but none greater than this—the presence of Jesus is real. Just like Nora discovered God at her lowest moment, so the disciples found Jesus when all their hopes were dashed.

Locked in a room filled with fear—Jesus is there. Weeping in a graveyard—Jesus is there. Filled with doubt—Jesus is there. Lying in a hospital bed—Jesus is there.

No matter what your circumstances, Jesus' promise holds true: "Never will I leave you, never will I forsake you." (HEBREWS 13:5)

*Because of the Resurrection...*

# 20

# YOU CAN STOP WORRYING

*"Do not be anxious about anything, but in everything, by prayer and petition, with thanksgiving, present your requests to God."*
PHILIPPIANS 4:6

*"Most Christians are being crucified on a cross between two thieves: yesterday's regret and tomorrow's worries."*
—WARREN WIERSBE

SEVERAL YEARS AGO, I preached a sermon titled, "Why Pray When You Can Worry?" The point was this: Worry is life's most useless activity. There are three huge problems with choosing anxiety as a lifestyle:

- **Worry doesn't work**— Jesus put it this way: "Who of you by worrying can add a single hour to his life?" (MATTHEW 6:27) Worrying cannot make me taller or smarter or lengthen my life. One person described worry this way: "Worry is like a rocking chair; it will give me something to do, but it won't get me anywhere." Worry can't change the past. Worry can't control the future. The only thing that worry can change is me—it makes me miserable in the present.

- **Worry is destructive**— Anxiety saps us of the emotional energy it takes to tackle the problems we worry about—like the hypochondriac who put on his tombstone, "I told you I was sick." Concentration-camp survivor Corrie Ten Boom put it this way: "Worry does not empty tomorrow of its sorrows; it empties today of its strength."

- **Worry dishonors God**— Jesus was even more forceful: "Why do you worry about clothes?" He asked. "See how the lilies of the field grow. They do not labor or spin. Yet I tell you that not even Solomon in all his splendor was dressed like one of these. If that is how God clothes the grass of the field, which is here today and tomorrow is thrown into the fire, will He not much more clothe you, O you of little faith?" (MATTHEW 6:28–30) Worry dishonors God because worry is practical atheism.

The Resurrection demonstrates that even in the darkest of circumstances God can still work. It is because of that assurance we can find freedom from anxiety as we begin to trust God. As George Muller said, "The beginning of anxiety is the end of faith, and the beginning of true faith is the end of anxiety."

*Because of the Resurrection...* **21**

# YOU CAN LET GO OF GUILT

*"Therefore there is now no condemnation*
*for those who are in Christ Jesus."*
ROMANS 8:1

THERE WERE TWO LITTLE BOYS, ages eight and ten, who could not stay out of trouble. Any mischief going on in their neighborhood, and everyone knew these boys were behind it. Exasperated, their mother called a local pastor, who had a reputation for getting children to behave, and asked if he would speak with her boys. He agreed but asked to see them individually.

The mother sent her eight-year-old in first that morning, with the older boy to see the pastor in the afternoon. The pastor, a huge man with a booming voice, sat the younger boy down and asked him sternly, "Where is God?"

The boy's mouth dropped open, but he made no response. He just sat there, with his mouth hanging open, his eyes bugging out.

The pastor repeated the question in a sterner tone. "Where is God?" he demanded.

Again, no answer.

Exasperated, the pastor shook his finger in the boy's face and bellowed, "Where is God?"

The boy screamed and bolted from the room, ran directly home, and dove into his closet, slamming the door behind him. When his older brother found him, he asked, "What happened?" The younger brother, gasping for breath, replied: "We are in big trouble this time. God is missing—and they think we did it!"

Peter could relate. He was in trouble, and he knew it. Jesus had told the disciples that He would be arrested, and that they would all abandon Him. Peter pledged allegiance, then he denied Jesus three times. Worst of all, during the last denial, Jesus had been looking right at him (LUKE 22:61).

Overcome, Peter did what most of us would do. He ran away.

Guilt can have that effect on us. By keeping us focused on past failures, it prevents us from moving forward. Guilt traps us in an endless cycle of failure, regret, and embarrassment.

The million-dollar question is this? How can I break free from guilt? Notice how Jesus therapeutically freed Peter from his guilt:

"When they had finished eating, Jesus said to Simon Peter, 'Simon, son of John, do you truly love Me more than these?' 'Yes, Lord,' he said, 'You know that I love You.' Jesus said, 'Feed My lambs.'

"Again Jesus said, 'Simon, son of John, do you truly love Me?' He answered, 'Yes, Lord, you know that I love You.' Jesus said, 'Take care of My sheep.' The third time He said to him, 'Simon, son of John, do you love Me?' Peter was hurt because Jesus asked him the third time, 'Do you love Me?' He said, 'Lord, You know all things; You know that I love You….' Then Jesus said to him, 'Follow Me!'" (JOHN 21:15–17)

Amazing! Jesus asked Peter three present-tense questions then gave him three future-tense assignments. Not one word about his past! Not one word about his failure! Jesus resolved and forgave his past and then brought Peter to the present and pointed him to the future. That is God's key to escaping the prison of guilt!

Maybe the Apostle Paul was thinking of this encounter when he penned this great guilt-destroying, life-giving prescription: "Forgetting what is behind and straining toward what is ahead, I press on toward the goal to win the prize for which God has called me heavenward in Christ Jesus." (PHILIPPIANS 3:13–14)

*Because of the Resurrection...*  **22**

# YOU CAN EXPERIENCE REAL PEACE

*"So when it was evening on that day, the first day of the week, and when the doors were shut where the disciples were, for fear of the Jews, Jesus came and stood in their midst and said to them, 'Peace be with you.' And when He had said this, He showed them both His hands and His side. The disciples then rejoiced when they saw the Lord. So Jesus said to them again, 'Peace be with you; as the Father has sent Me, I also send you.'"*
JOHN 20:19–21

*"Let the peace of Christ rule in your hearts, since as members of one body you were called to peace. And be thankful."*
COLOSSIANS 3:15

WHEN SHE WAS NINE YEARS OLD, Mary Taylor Previte was taken captive in China, where she was living with her missionary parents, and put in a Japanese POW camp. She spent three years in the camp and was separated from her parents for even longer. "We saw a lot of weapons, a lot of blood, and I didn't see my parents for five and a half years," she said.

That kind of trauma could haunt a child for years and leave her constantly fearful, unable to find real peace. But in her book, *Hungry Ghosts*, Mary said she found strength in the prison camps. "We were surrounded by teachers who instilled in us the profound belief that we had a future," she said. "They made us memorize Bible verses about the purpose and power of God. They convinced us that God would protect us. They taught us that 'all things work together for good for them that love the Lord.' They taught us that even in the concentration camp, something good was going to happen."

"God had led His people to the Promised Land and had done miracles, closed the mouth of lions, raised Jesus and now guess what? We were next!" she said. "Our teachers filled our heads with these positive images, and in the middle of violence, of war, surrounded by guard dogs, bayonets, and electric wires, we felt safe."

Years later, Mary would become director of Camden County Youth Center in New Jersey, where children arrested for violent crimes were held before standing trial. A hopeless, violent facility when she arrived, the center was transformed into a place where those broken children could be restored. She had experienced God's peace in a POW camp; now she brings that peace into the lives of children in a New Jersey prison.

The world offers us another kind of peace. Some people look for peace by drinking enough to become numb. Others search for peace in one relationship after another, hoping someone will fill the void in their lives. Some people try to find peace in busyness or possessions, and come up empty every time.

- **Real peace** is found in knowing Jesus Christ, God's Son.

- **Real peace** means knowing that no matter what I do, God will not stop loving me.

- **Real peace** is knowing that no matter what happens in the future, God will give me strength to handle it.

- **Real peace** means that my life and my family are safe in God's hands.

The Apostle Paul told us this in Philippians 4:5–7: "The Lord is near. Do not be anxious about anything, but in everything, by prayer and petition, with thanksgiving, present your requests to God. And the peace of God, which transcends all understanding, will guard your hearts and your minds in Christ Jesus."

That's real peace!

*Because of the Resurrection...*  **23**

# YOU CAN EXPECT GREAT THINGS FROM GOD

*"For nothing is impossible with God."*

LUKE 1:37

IN 1939, A DOCTORAL STUDENT named George Bernard Dantzig arrived late for Professor Jerzy Neyman's graduate statistics class at the University of California, Berkeley. On the board were two mathematical problems, which Dantzig assumed were homework assignments. He wrote them down in his notebook and spent the next few days trying to solve them.

"A few days later," Dantzig told the College Mathematics Journal, "I apologized to Neyman for taking so long to do the homework — the problems seemed to be a little harder than usual. I asked him if he still wanted it. He told me to throw it on his desk. I did so reluctantly because his desk was covered with such a heap of papers that I feared my homework would be lost there forever."

Six weeks later, Dantzig was awakened at home on a Sunday morning by someone pounding on his front door. It was Professor Neyman. "He rushed in with papers in hand, all excited," Dantzig recalled. It turned out that Dantzig had made a mistake. The problems on the blackboard hadn't been homework assignments at all. They were two famed "unsolvable problems"—which had baffled mathematicians for years.

Years later, Dantzig admitted that if he'd known the problems were "unsolvable," he would have given up trying. Instead, because he expected to solve them, he kept working at them until he did.

The Bible is full of people who defied expectations. No one thought that David stood a chance against Goliath. No one gave Moses half a chance of setting his people free. No one expected Jesus to walk out of the grave on Easter Sunday. But David slew Goliath, Moses freed the Israelites, and Jesus rose from the grave, proving nothing is impossible—with God.

No one expected much of William Carey, either. Born in 1761, he spent most of his early career as a shoemaker in England. He had little education, little money, and no influence. But one day, while out walking, he starting thinking about Jesus' command to go into the whole world and preach the Good News. "Surely," he thought to himself, "Jesus meant what He said." He decided that he would go to India as a missionary.

His pastor thought otherwise. "Sit down, young man, sit down and be still," his pastor told him. "When God wants to convert the heathen, He will do it without consulting either you or me." (At this time in history, churches had given up on sending out missionaries.)

Carey refused to give up. He studied to become a minister, kept praying, and never gave up on his dream. "Expect great things from God! Attempt great things for God!" became his motto. Finally, in 1792 he set sail for India, where he founded a school, became an expert on the local Bengali language, and led thousands to Christ. He translated the Bible into Bengali and started a movement to end the practice of "sati," or widow burnings. Tens of thousands of missionaries would follow his example, taking the message of Jesus all over the world.

Expect great things from God. Attempt great things for God. Because the Resurrection reminds us nothing is impossible with God.

*Because of the Resurrection...*

# 24

# YOU CAN EXPERIENCE HOPE

*"For I know the plans I have for you," declares*
*the Lord, "plans to prosper you and not to harm*
*you, plans to give you hope and a future."*
JEREMIAH 29:11

JOSEPH HAD HIGH HOPES. Handsome and smart, he was his father's favorite. He also had dreams, which often came true. One night, he dreamt that all 11 of his brothers would bow down before him and follow him. This did not go over very well with his brothers. They sold him into slavery (a solution many parents of teenagers have contemplated).

Being sold into slavery was only the beginning of Joseph's troubles. When he refused to have an affair with his master's wife, she accused him of trying to assault her. Joseph was tossed in jail. He remained there for years, with no hope of ever getting out.

Then, his big break came. Pharaoh was haunted by nightmares and needed someone who could interpret them, but no one could. Finally, Pharaoh's cook, who'd been in jail with Joseph years earlier, mentioned Joseph to his boss. The cook knew about Joseph's knack for interpreting dreams. Soon, Joseph was led before Pharaoh. When he correctly interpreted the dream, telling Pharaoh that seven years of famine were on the way (GENESIS 41:15–32), Pharaoh responded by making Joseph his right-hand man and putting him in charge of famine preparations.

Through all the years of suffering, Joseph's hope never failed. As a gospel song puts it, "in the midnight hour" God turned things around.

Time and again in the Bible, God did great things through people who suffered but never lost hope. Many times, God acted when things seemed at their darkest.

- **Before Abraham became the father of many nations —he and Sarah were childless.**

- **Before Moses led Israel out of Egypt —he was a fugitive running for his life.**

- **Before David was anointed king —he was rejected by his family.**

- **Before Hosea became a powerful spokesman for God —his wife betrayed him.**

- **Before Peter preached before thousands —he denied his Savior three times.**

All of these people found hope in their darkest hour. Hope is a powerful word. Hope helps us keep going through our toughest battles. Hope helps us climb over obstacles when others have given up. One writer describes hope this way: "Hope is believing, in spite of the evidence, then watching the evidence change."

Because of the Resurrection, we have hope. Hope that God is always with us. Hope for a better future, no matter what our present circumstances. Hope that death itself has been defeated.

C.S. Lewis said that the hope of heaven isn't "a form of escapism or wishful thinking." Because Christians have hope, he said, they refuse to accept the world the way it is.

"If you read history," Lewis wrote in *Mere Christianity*, "you will find that the Christians who did most for the present world were just those who thought most of the next. It is since Christians have largely ceased to think of the other world that they have become so ineffective in this. Aim at heaven, and you will get earth thrown in. Aim at earth, and you will get neither."

*Because of the Resurrection...*  **25**

# YOU CAN EXPERIENCE THE REALITY OF THE CROSS

*"For the message of the cross is foolishness to those who are perishing, but to us who are being saved it is the power of God."*
1 CORINTHIANS 1:18

JEFFREY EBERT was five years old when he first learned the true meaning of love. He was sitting on his mother's lap, enjoying a late-night ride home in the family car. (This was before mandatory seat-belts and car seats.) Suddenly, a drunk driver in the opposite lane lost control of his car. He swerved and hit the Eberts head on.

After the collision, Jeffrey woke up, covered in blood. Writing about the crash in *Leadership* magazine, he said, "Then I learned that the blood wasn't mine at all, but my mother's. In that split second when two headlights glared into her eyes, she instinctively pulled me closer to her chest and curled her body around mine. It was her body that slammed against the dashboard, her head that shattered the windshield. She took the impact of the collision so I didn't have to."

Jeffrey Ebert's mother survived but was critically injured. He never forgot his mother's love, how she put herself in harm's way for him. Without his mother's sacrifice, Jeffrey would have been killed.

That's the message of the cross. Christ loved us so much that He was willing to die, so that we could live. The cross is a place of redemption and a place of relationship. Jesus told His disciples, "greater love has no one, than he who lays down his life for his friends." (JOHN 15:13)

In *The Green Mile,* a movie based on Stephen King's book, Tom Hanks plays Paul Edgecomb, head guard on death row at the Cold Mountain Prison. One day, a new prisoner arrives. John Coffey, played by Michael Clarke Duncan, is a giant, close to seven feet tall. A quiet, gentle man, Coffey was falsely convicted of murder. He also has a mysterious gift—he can heal people by literally absorbing their illnesses. Early in the film, Edgecomb suffers from a bad infection, and with just one touch from Coffey he is cured.

When Edgecomb learns that the warden's wife, a dear friend, has an inoperable brain tumor, he and other guards sneak Coffey out of the prison on a midnight run to the warden's house. As guards escort John into the house, they hear the warden's wife screaming in agony. Once a kind and loving woman, she has been reduced to a mere shell, driven mad with pain.

John approaches the warden's wife slowly. She asks his name, and he tells her, "John Coffey, ma'am. Just like the drink but not spelled the same." They talk for a few minutes, and then he leans over her. "I see it," he says. Suddenly he takes her hands and places his mouth near hers. A stream of black bugs, representing the cancer, flies from her body and into Coffey's. The room becomes bright, and the house begins to shake. Suddenly, all becomes quiet. The warden's wife is completely changed: The disease has left her body, and she's returned to normal. John falls over and begins to cough loudly. He has taken her sickness upon himself.

The warden's wife was made whole because John absorbed the pain. From the Bible's vantage point, that is precisely what Jesus did during His passion at Calvary.

He took your pain upon Himself and offers you the gifts of forgiveness, wholeness, and new life.

*Because of the Resurrection...*  **26**

# YOU CAN KNOW GOD PERSONALLY

*"What is more, I consider everything a loss compared to the surpassing greatness of knowing Christ Jesus my Lord...."*
PHILIPPIANS 3:8

ONE SATURDAY MORNING, a pastor decided to pay a visit to some of his church members. When he got to one house, the lights were on, and he heard sounds inside, so it was clear someone was home. But though he knocked several times, no one answered. He left his card at the door with a Bible verse, Revelation 3:20: "Behold, I stand at the door and knock. If anyone hears My voice and opens the door, I will come in to him and dine with him, and him with Me."

The next day at church, the card turned up in the collection plate. Below the pastor's message was another Bible verse, Genesis 3:10: "I heard your voice in the garden, and I was afraid because I was naked, and I hid myself."

A lot of people are hiding from God these days. Only about one in five Americans shows up at church each week, even though surveys tell us that 90% of Americans believe in God and that many of them want to have a personal relationship with Him.

But that is exactly why Jesus Christ came! He didn't come to launch a religious system, filled with rules and regulations. He came so that everyone could have a thriving, personal relationship with God through Him. The central message of the Bible and the core reason for Christ's birth, death, and Resurrection is this: You were created to enjoy a personal relationship with God!

Here are some of the things that God offers us, through a relationship with Jesus Christ:

- **Complete forgiveness.** (1 JOHN 1:9)

- **A clean slate and fresh start.** (2 CORINTHIANS 5:17)

- **The gift of eternal life.** (JOHN 3:16)

- **Freedom from guilt.** (ROMANS 8:1)

- **Freedom from fear.** (2 TIMOTHY 1:7)

- **God's power in my life.** (PHILIPPIANS 4:1)

- **God's presence in my life.** (JOSHUA 1:5)

- **God's principles to live by.** (2 TIMOTHY 3:16–17)

- **God's people for encouragement.** (HEBREWS 10:24–25)

- **God's purpose for life.** (COLOSSIANS 1:28–29)

More importantly, we can know that God cares for us and will never abandon us, no matter what happens. In *The Four Pillars of a Man's Heart*, Stu Weber tells of a family who were on vacation, relaxing in a cabin by a beautiful lake. While the dad worked on an old boat, his young son and daughter played on the pier. The little boy lost his balance and fell in the water, causing his sister to scream in panic. The father heard the scream, saw the splash, and knew instantly what had happened.

Without hesitating, he sprinted to the end of the pier and dove into the water, frantically searching for his son. He found the boy under the water, holding on tightly to one of the wooden beams that supported the pier. He grabbed his son and swam to the surface.

Safely on shore, through tears of joy and relief, he asked: "Son, why were you holding on to the pier? Why didn't you just let go and float to the surface?"

The boy said, "I didn't need to, Daddy. I knew you would come for me."

"When you feel like you can't hold on any longer," Weber says, "when God's answers seem to be a long time in coming, get a fresh grip on hope, because He is faithful."

*Because of the Resurrection...*

# 27

# YOU CAN RECEIVE COMPLETE FORGIVENESS

*"Jesus, remember me when you come into Your kingdom."*
LUKE 23:42

JESUS WAS DYING. Nailed to the cross, He experienced inconceivable agony. Even at the last moments of His life, He reached out with God's love and forgiveness. One of the thieves crucified next to Jesus begged for forgiveness, and Jesus granted it, immediately. "Today," He told the thief, "you will be with Me in Paradise." (LUKE 23:41)

In life, we don't often get much grace. Most of the time, our experience is like that of Dave Hagler. Hagler, a writer who used to umpire local baseball games, was once stopped for speeding near Boulder, CO. He tried, without much luck, to talk the officer out of giving him a ticket. In a piece that appeared in the *Los Angeles Times*, Hagler said he told the officer "how worried I was about my insurance going up and what a careful driver I normally was. I begged him for grace. I begged him."

The officer ignored Hagler's pleas. He wrote up the ticket, handed it to Hagler, and told him if he didn't like it, he could "go to court."

"The first game of the next baseball season," Hagler wrote, "I was umpiring behind home plate, and the first batter up was (you guessed it) that same policeman. I recognized him, and he recognized me. He nervously asked me, 'How did things go with your ticket?' I just stared at him, and then I told him, 'Swing at everything!'"

Easter is God's invitation to experience grace, forgiveness, and a brand new start! How important is this? Paul said nothing is more important: "For what I received I passed on to you as of first importance: that Christ died for our sins according to the Scriptures." (1 CORINTHIANS 15:3–4)

Living in a prison of resentment and regret, trapped by bitterness and paralyzed by past mistakes, is no way to live! Maybe you've felt like that. Maybe you've felt like Humpty Dumpty: "Nothing could put me back together again." You're wrong. God specializes in new beginnings. That's what Easter is all about. "When someone becomes a Christian he becomes a new person inside. He is not the same anymore. A new life has begun." (2 CORINTHIANS 5:17)

Many of us don't believe that God can forgive us. We stay trapped in the past. We can't enjoy the present or dream about the future. We are haunted by what might have been.

Are you holding on to a past hurt? Perhaps you failed, falling flat on your face, and are still haunted by the embarrassment you felt. Maybe you had an abusive relationship in the past and still carry the scars. Maybe your parents or your spouse rejected you, and you can't believe that anyone would ever love you for who you are.

There's good news. God can set you free from the prison of resentment and heal you from the poison of regret. At Easter, Jesus took our pain and our failures, and carried them to the cross. With His suffering and death, He wiped all of our slates clean.

Then, on Easter Sunday, He stepped out of the grave and invited us to follow in His footsteps. The book of Hebrews tells us that Jesus knows our weaknesses and failings and still accepts us. "Let us then approach the throne of grace with confidence that we may receive mercy and find grace to help us in our time of need." (HEBREWS 4:16)

When we sin, when things go wrong, our first impulse is to hide from God. But because of Easter we can run to God, and He will forgive us.

We don't need to be afraid of God. The Bible says that Jesus, Who lived and died and rose again for our sakes, calls us His friends.

*Because of the Resurrection...* **28**

# YOU CAN KNOW DEATH IS DEFEATED

*"Even though I walk through the valley of the shadow
of death, I will fear no evil, for You are with me;
Your rod and Your staff, they comfort me."*
PSALM 23:4

*"This life is only the title page for eternity as a Christian."*
—C.S. LEWIS

I HEARD A STORY OF A WOMAN caught in a frightening storm in the middle of the Atlantic. She kept all the children from panicking by telling them Bible stories. After reaching port safely, the ship's captain approached the woman and said, "How in the world did you remain calm when everyone else was afraid the ship would sink?" She said: "I have two daughters. One in New York, one in heaven. Either way, I knew I would see one of my daughters in a few hours, and it really didn't matter to me which one." That's the type of calm confidence promised by Jesus Christ and available to every believer.

"Jesus said... 'I am the Resurrection and the Life. He who believes in Me will live, even though he dies; and whoever lives and believes in Me will never die. Do you believe this?'" (JOHN 11:25–26)

As a pastor, I often read the following at memorial services: A couple in their eighties died in a car crash. They had been in good health, as the wife had insisted on eating only health food and getting plenty of exercise.

When they reached the pearly gates, St. Peter took them to a mansion, decked out with a beautiful kitchen, master bath suite, and backyard Jacuzzi.

The husband told St. Peter, "We love the house, but how much is it going to cost?"

"It's free," Peter replied. "This is heaven."

Next, they went out back and saw the championship golf course. They would have golfing privileges every day, and each week the course changed to a new one that put the great golf courses on earth to shame.

"What are the green fees?" the husband asked.

"This is heaven," Peter said. "You play for free."

Next, they went to the club house and saw a lavish buffet with the cuisines of the world laid out. "How much is it to eat here?" the old man asked.

"Don't you understand yet?" St. Peter said. "This is heaven. It's free!"

"Well, where are the low-fat and low-cholesterol foods?" the old man asked timidly. "That's the best part," Peter explained. "You can eat as much as you like, of whatever you like, and never get fat. This is heaven!"

The old man looked at his wife and said: "You and your darned bran muffins! I could have been here 10 years ago!"

I'm not sure that there are golf courses and all-you-can-eat buffets in heaven. But that story captures an essential truth. God promises us eternal life through the death and Resurrection of His Son, Jesus. Eternal life is better than anything we could hope or imagine. Christians live forever in the joy of God's presence.

In *The Last Battle*, the final book in *The Chronicles of Narnia*, C.S. Lewis painted a picture of what eternal life is like. At the end of the book, the children learn they can't go back to earth from the enchanted land of Narnia. They have died, the great lion Aslan tells them. Now, they can remain with him forever.

"The term is over," he tells them. "The holidays have begun. The dream is ended: This is the morning."

Rather than being filled with sorrow, the children experience overwhelming joy. "And as he spoke he no longer looked to them like a lion," Lewis wrote, "but the things that began to happen after that are so great and so beautiful that I cannot write them. And for us this is the end of all the stories, and we can most truly say that they all lived happily ever after. But for them it was only the beginning of the real story. All of their lives and their adventures in Narnia had been only the cover and the title page; now at last they were beginning Chapter One of the great story, which no one on earth has ever read, in which every chapter is better than the one before."

*Because of the Resurrection...* **29**

# YOU CAN LIVE WITH ETERNAL VALUES

*"For me, to live is Christ, and to die is gain."*
PHILIPPIANS 1:21

WHEN JESUS WANTED TO MAKE A POINT, He usually didn't give a lecture. Instead, He told a story, also known as a parable. Here's a parable for our time:

*A policeman arrived at the scene of an accident before the dust had even settled. He found that a wealthy young man had been thrown clear just before his Mercedes plunged over a steep cliff and crashed onto the rocks, far below, in a ball of flames. The young man was standing along the roadside at the top of the cliff, weeping, and bleeding profusely from the stump at his shoulder, all that was left of his arm.*

*"My Mercedes! My Mercedes!" the young man howled.*

*"You ought to be thankful you're alive," the amazed policeman said.*

*"But it had twenty thousand dollars' worth of options," the man whimpered, staring down at the burning wreckage.*

*"There are things more important than that stupid car," the policeman insisted, guiding the injured man away from the cliff. "We've got to get you to a hospital. Your arm has been torn off, you could bleed to death!"*

*The young man looked down and noticed for the first time that his arm was missing. Horrified, he screamed, "My Rolex! My Rolex!"*

An exaggeration? Not by much. Today's headlines are full of stories of people who destroy their lives out of fear of losing their material possessions. They murder to collect insurance policies, defraud to build business empires, and steal to accumulate what they cannot keep. They are willing to risk their lives to gain things, but fear prevents them from risking their things to gain life.

The Resurrection shows that anything that does not have eternal value is eternally out of date. It's like building a nest in a tree you know is going to be chopped down tomorrow. Here today, gone tomorrow.

Perhaps no one understood that as well as Francesco Bernardone, better known as St. Francis of Assisi. The son of a wealthy merchant, he hoped to follow his father into business and live a life of luxury. Then, one day, while walking by a ruined church, he heard Jesus speak to him: "Francis, repair My falling house." Francis went and sold some silk from his father's storehouse to pay for repairing the church. His father thought it was a waste of money and demanded that Francis come to his senses. When Francis refused, his father disowned him. Rather than walk away from God, Francis gave back all his possessions, even the clothes on his back.

Francis had too much to live on and not enough to live for. So he gave it all up, restored the church, and became one of the most beloved Christians in history.

In his book, *Death by Suburb*, Dave Goetz said, "Too much of the good life ends up being toxic, deforming us spiritually." Instead of the good life, Goetz said, "God offers us the thicker life, a life full of meaning and purpose."

Eugene Peterson described that well in his paraphrase of Jesus in Matthew, Chapter 11: "Are you tired? Worn out? Burned out on religion? Come to Me. Get away with Me and you'll recover your life. I'll show you how to take a real rest. Walk with Me and work with Me, watch how I do it. Learn the unforced rhythms of grace. I won't lay anything heavy or ill-fitting on you. Keep company with Me, and you'll learn to live freely and lightly." (MATTHEW 11:28–30, *The Message*)

C.S. Lewis, in his essay, "The Weight of Glory," reminded us that the only thing in this world that lasts forever is people—who were made in God's image, and meant to live forever. "There are no ordinary people," he wrote. "You have never talked to a mere mortal. Nations, cultures, arts, civilization, these are mortal, and their life is to ours as the life of a gnat. But it is immortals whom we joke with, work with, marry, snub, and exploit."

Anything that is not eternal is eternally out of date.

*Because of the Resurrection...* **30**

# YOU CAN KNOW THAT JESUS CHRIST IS ALIVE

*"In their fright the women bowed down with their faces to the ground, but the men said to them, 'Why do you look for the living among the dead? He is not here; He has risen!'"*

LUKE 24:5–6

IN NOVEMBER 2001, inspired by the Arizona Diamondbacks coming from behind to beat the Yankees in the World Series, the editors of *Sports Illustrated* put together a Top Ten list of famous comebacks. Elvis Presley made the list, as did Michael Jordan and Muhammad Ali. Harry Truman, who defeated Thomas Dewey in the 1948 presidential election, even though the *Chicago Tribune* declared Dewey the winner, made the list as well. Two countries, Japan and Germany, were on the list, as was "humanity" for surviving the Black Plague, which killed 25 million people during the 14th century.

Who was №. 1 in the all-time comeback list? Jesus Christ. "Defies critics and stuns the Romans with His Resurrection," the editors of *Sports Illustrated* wrote.

There were many would-be messiahs in Israel, before and after Jesus. The story was always the same. They would get a few follow-ers and start causing trouble. At some point, they'd go too far and do something that caught the attention of the Romans. Then the Roman soldiers would come in and crush them, bringing a swift end to the false messiah and his followers. No one ever came back against the Romans.

Except for Jesus. On Easter, two days after He had been crucified, Jesus rose from the dead. And the movement that the Romans believed they had crushed sprang back to life with Him. Three hundred years later, even the Roman emperor would bow down and worship Jesus Christ. Small wonder the Resurrection is considered the greatest comeback of all time. Nothing else comes close.

There are some modern theologians who think the Resurrection never happened. These theologians believe that, when the early Christians said Jesus rose from the dead, they were speaking metaphorically. But that explanation doesn't add up.

In *Knowing the Truth About the Resurrection,* William Craig tells the story of two boys joking about canceling Easter:

"There ain't gonna be no Easter this year," one of them says.

"Why not?" the other asks.

"They found the body," his friend replies.

These two boys knew the truth, Craig says. Without the Resurrection, Christianity is worthless.

"And if Christ had not been raised," the Apostle Paul said, "then our preaching is vain, your faith also is vain. If we have hoped in Christ in this life only, we are of all men most to be pitied." (1 CORINTHIANS 15:14)

The truth is, something caused the birth of a worldwide movement 2,000 years ago, a movement that turned the world upside down. The early church was fueled by the enthusiasm of people who one minute had been cowards about the future and days later were changing the future. The only explanation that fits: They had seen the Resurrection. Jesus rose from the dead.

In John, Chapter 11, Jesus heard that His friend Lazarus was ill. But by the time He arrived, it was too late. Jesus arrived to find Lazarus' sisters, Mary and Martha, in mourning; their brother was dead. Jesus said a very strange thing to Martha: "I am the Resurrection and the Life. He who believes in Me will live, even though he dies; and whoever lives and believes in Me will never die." (JOHN 11:25)

Then He asked, "Do you believe this?"

When Martha said yes, Jesus walked to the grave where Lazarus was buried. First, He wept for His friend, then He raised Lazarus from the dead.

"I am the Resurrection and the Life," Jesus said.

Do you believe? That is the question of the ages!

# 31

# EVIDENCE FOR THE RESURRECTION

*"And if Christ has not been raised, our preaching is useless and so is your faith."*
1 CORINTHIANS 15:14

*"Christianity does not hold the Resurrection to be one among many tenets of belief. Without faith in the Resurrection there would be no Christianity at all. The Christian church would never have begun and the Jesus movement would have fizzled.... Christianity stands or falls with the truth of the Resurrection. Once you disprove it, you have disposed of Christianity."*
—MICHAEL GREEN, *MAN ALIVE*

AS I MENTIONED in the introduction to this book, I grew up in a family of skeptics. And when it came to Christianity's greatest claim, the Resurrection, I had serious doubts. I was skeptical about stories claiming a dead man had come back to life. I was skeptical about claims that the tomb was actually empty on that first Easter morning. I was skeptical that accounts of people who claimed to encounter a risen Christ were credible. I was impressed by the sincerity of Christians who believed that He rose from the dead, but I was convinced they were sincerely misguided. If these doubts sound familiar, then read on.

The following pages detail the evidence that replaced my skepticism with confident faith.

## A Brief History

In 66 AD, outraged that the Roman governor Florus had been stealing from the temple in Jerusalem, the Israelites revolted. Led by generals like Simon bar Goria, whom some thought could be the Messiah, they defeated the Roman garrison in Jerusalem. When the Roman governor of Syria, Cestius Gallus, sent in reinforcements, they were defeated, as well. Tens of thousands joined the rebel army. Finally, it seemed, God would deliver Israel from the Roman occupation.

Four years later, Jerusalem lay in ruins. The temple was destroyed. As many as 100,000 people were killed or carried off into slavery. The revolt was crushed. Simon and other rebels were taken to Rome, where they were paraded in front of crowds and then put to death.

Now, said N.T. Wright, a leading New Testament scholar, suppose that several followers of Simon, hiding from the Roman army, were to go around saying that Simon really was the Messiah. Then suppose that, despite all the evidence, they went around claiming that Simon, and not the Roman emperor, was lord of the whole world.

Anyone who heard them would think they had lost their minds. Wright said, "The verdict of madness, of a kind of criminal lunacy, which turns reality upside down and inside out, seems inevitable."

Yet that is exactly what the followers of Jesus did. After Jesus was crucified, His followers began preaching that He was the Christ—the Lord of the world, and the Son of God. But instead of calling them mad, thousands of people believed the disciples.

Why? Because the disciples claimed that Jesus was raised from the dead. They testified that they had been to Jesus' tomb, and it was empty. Jesus had appeared to them, walked with them, even eaten with them. Then He had sent them out to tell the whole world that He was the Son of God.

Without this claim that Jesus rose from the dead, Wright argued in his 750-page book, *The Resurrection of the Son of God*, there is no Christianity. Either the disciples were telling the truth, or they were mad. For more than 2,000 years, the witness to the Resurrection of Jesus Christ has forced people to choose one of these two alternatives.

Throughout the centuries, Christians have held the position that there is plenty of evidence to convince rational, unbiased, thinking people that Jesus did, in fact, rise from the dead. Is this still true today? Can a 21st-century-thinking American still believe that the Resurrection really happened?

## Eyewitness Testimony

One of the earliest Christian statements about the Resurrection is found in 1 Corinthians, where the Apostle Paul repeats one of the earliest creeds (or statements of faith) of the church. "For what I received I passed on to you as of first importance: that Christ died for our sins according to the Scriptures, that He was buried, that He was raised on the third day according to the Scriptures, and that He appeared to Peter, and then to the Twelve. After that, He appeared to more than five hundred of the brothers at the same time, most of whom are still living, though some have fallen asleep." (1 CORINTHIANS 5:3–6)

In his book, *The Case for Christ*, Lee Strobel interviewed two New Testament scholars, Dr. Craig Bloomberg and Dr. William Lane Craig, who pointed out that Paul met with Peter and other disciples within two years of the Resurrection. Paul heard testimony from eyewitnesses, who were using this statement—Jesus was crucified, buried, and born again—to summarize their faith. Bloomberg pointed out that modern scholars, like Karen Armstrong—who argue that the Resurrection was a myth invented decades after Jesus' death—ignore this crucial piece of evidence.

Paul also is saying this in 1 Corinthians:

- The Resurrection of Jesus didn't happen in secret.

- Jesus was seen by large numbers of people in different locations, at different times, and in different circumstances over a 40-day period.

- Most of the people who saw Jesus were still alive when Paul was writing, so his testimony could be verified.

## The Accuracy of the New Testament

The late F.F. Bruce, who was a New Testament scholar at the University of Manchester, pointed out that "if the New Testament were a collection of secular writings, their authenticity would generally be regarded as beyond all doubt." For example, Craig Bloomberg told Lee Strobel that the earliest biographies of Alexander the Great were written more than 400 years after Alexander's death, "yet historians consider them to be generally trustworthy." The earliest accounts of Jesus' life, by comparison, were written within 30 or 40 years of His death.

Josh McDowell, who spent years trying to disprove the New Testament, finally accepted it as historically accurate—in part because so many ancient copies of it exist. "If one discards the Bible as being unreliable," he wrote in *Evidence That Demands a Verdict*, "then he must discard almost all literature of antiquity."

## The Alternate Theories Don't Hold Up

For nearly 2,000 years, skeptics have come up with ways to explain away the Resurrection and the empty tomb. But under close examination not one of these alternatives holds up.

## ALTERNATIVE # 1: JESUS DIDN'T REALLY DIE

This alternative speculates that Jesus didn't die on the cross. Instead, shock from the loss of blood on the cross and from the beating Jesus endured sent Jesus into a coma. When He was placed in the tomb, the coolness of the stone and the aroma of the burial spices revived Him. When He came out of the grave, the disciples assumed that He was resurrected. A second version of this story, popularized in Hugh Schonfield's book, *Passover Plot*, argues that Jesus faked His death by being drugged on the cross. He then revived and walked out of the tomb.

But this theory falls apart when examined closely. First of all, the Romans crucified thousands of people. As the film *The Passion of the Christ* illustrated, Roman soldiers were brutal, efficient, and merciless when it came to crucifixion. They would not be fooled by a coma caused by loss of blood or by drugs. They had a vested interest in making sure Jesus was dead. The account of Jesus' death in the Gospel of John included this detail: a Roman soldier thrust a spear into Jesus' side, and a gush of water and blood came out. Modern medicine explains this detail—the spear pierced the pericardium, the covering of the heart. When a person dies, the pericardium fills with a clear fluid. The spear went through the pericardium and into the heart, causing a flow of water and blood.

## ALTERNATIVE # 2: THE STOLEN BODY THEORY

This alternative argues that the disciples, or someone else, stole the body. But who had the means and the motive to steal the body? Not the Romans or the Jewish authorities—they wanted Jesus dead. Had they taken the body, they could have produced it and then snuffed out the Christian church in its infancy. Even the disciples seemed unlikely suspects. They would have been little match for the Roman guards at the tomb. Also, they had little to gain by lying about the missing body. Put yourself in their shoes: "OK, we're going to steal the body, and then we're going to lie and claim the body was resurrected.

Then, we're going to have the unspeakable privilege of living as penniless evangelists, wandering around the rest of our lives, being beaten, whipped, thrown in jail, and put to death." (Anyone reading this want to sign up?) All of the disciples were put to death, many by crucifixion, for testifying that Jesus rose from the grave. People will die for their faith if they believe that it is true. But people will not die for their faith if they know it's false.

## ALTERNATIVE # 3: THE WRONG TOMB THEORY

Another popular theory has been that the women, distraught and overcome by grief, missed their way in the darkness of the morning and went to the wrong tomb. In their distress they *imagined* Christ had risen because the tomb was empty. This theory, however, fails before the same fact that eliminates the previous one. If the women went to the wrong tomb, why did the high priests and other enemies of the faith not go to the right tomb and produce the body? Further, it is inconceivable that all Jesus' followers would succumb to the same mistake, and certainly Joseph of Arimathea, owner of the tomb, would have solved the problem. In addition, it must be remembered that this was a private burial ground, not a public cemetery. There was no other tomb nearby that would have allowed them to make this mistake.

## ALTERNATIVE # 4: THE HALLUCINATION THEORY

This theory argues that the disciples wanted to see Jesus so badly that they imagined He rose from the grave. In essence, they had a hallucination in which they saw Jesus.

However, this theory also fails under scrutiny. For one, hallucinations are not group events. A psychologist has noted that 500 different people having the same hallucination at exactly the same time would be a greater miracle than the Resurrection itself.

## The Miracle of the Church

One of the greatest proofs of the Resurrection is the existence of the church. There were many would-be Messiahs before and after Jesus. The Romans arrested them, crucified them, and in doing so crushed their followers. All these other so-called Messiahs stayed dead. Their followers disappeared.

For a while, that's what everyone, including the disciples, thought would happen with Jesus. The disciples weren't expecting the Resurrection. After Jesus' death, they scattered. They were crushed. They hid in an upper room in Jerusalem and waited for their doom.

After the Resurrection, the disciples were transformed. In Acts, Peter, who had once denied Jesus because he was afraid of a woman servant, proclaimed to thousands that Jesus had come back from the dead. "Men of Israel, listen to this," he said. "Jesus of Nazareth was a man accredited by God to you by miracles, wonders, and signs, which God did among you through Him, as you yourselves know. This man was handed over to you by God's set purpose and foreknowledge; and you, with the help of wicked men, put Him to death by nailing Him to the cross. But God raised Him from the dead, freeing Him from the agony of death, because it was impossible for death to keep its hold on Him." (ACTS 2:22–24)

In response, no one said, "I don't know what they're talking about; I never saw any signs or miracles." No one said, "I've never heard of Jesus." Instead, history shows that 3,000 people responded by becoming followers of Jesus Christ. They knew Peter was speaking the truth. They knew the reality of Jesus's death and Resurrection and why these things had taken place in their midst.

As John R.W. Stott said, "The transformation of the disciples is perhaps the greatest evidence of all for the Resurrection".

## The Transformation of the Disciples

What was it that changed a band of frightened, cowardly disciples into men of courage and conviction? What was it that changed Peter? What was it 50 days later that enabled Peter to risk his life by saying he had seen Jesus risen from the dead.

What was it that changed Thomas' doubt and skepticism into a confident faith?

## The Evidence of Fulfilled Prophecy

During my years of skepticism, the evidence of fulfilled prophecy proved most troublesome. I realized I had no answer when faced with the literally scores of predictions that had been fulfilled, many written hundreds of years before Christ's time!

Some of the many prophesies about His death and Resurrection:

- He would ride into Jerusalem on a donkey.
  (ZECHARIAH 9:9)
- He would enter the temple.
  (MALACHI 3:1)
- He would be betrayed by a friend.
  (PSALM 41:9)
- He would be sold for 30 pieces of silver.
  (ZECHARIAH 11:12)
- The silver would be thrown into the temple.
  (ZECHARIAH 11:13)
- The silver would be used for the Potter's Field.
  (ZECHARIAH 11:13)
- He would be forsaken by His disciples.
  (ZECHARIAH 13:7)
- He would be accused by false witnesses.
  (PSALM 35:11)

- He would remain silent before accusers.
  (ISAIAH 53:7)
- He would be wounded and bruised.
  (ISAIAH 53:5)
- He would be whipped and spit upon.
  (ISAIAH 50:6, MICAH 5:1)
- He would be mocked.
  (PSALM 22:7,8)
- His hands and feet would be pierced.
  (PSALM 22:16)
- He would be crucified with thieves.
  (ISAIAH 53:12)
- People would shake their heads at Him.
  (PSALM 109:25)
- His clothes would be divided and lots cast for them.
  (PSALM 22:18)
- He would be offered gall and vinegar to drink.
  (PSALM 69:21)
- Not one of His bones would be broken.
  (PSALM 34:20)
- His heart would literally burst.
  (PSALM 22:14)
- His side would be pierced.
  (ZECHARIAH 12:10)
- Darkness would fall in broad daylight.
  (AMOS 8:9)
- He would be buried in a rich man's tomb.
  (ISAIAH 53:9)
- He would be resurrected from the dead.
  (PSALM 16:10, 30:3, 41:10. 118:17, HOSEA 6:2)

In his book, *Science Speaks,* Peter Stoner applies the modern science of probability to just eight prophecies regarding Christ. He says,

"The chance that any man might have fulfilled all eight prophecies is one in 10 to the 17th. That would be one in 100,000,000,000,000,000" Stoner suggests that "we take 10 to the 17th silver dollars and lay them on the face of Texas. They will cover all of the state two feet deep. Now mark one of these silver dollars and stir the whole mass thoroughly.... Blindfold a man and tell him he can travel as far as he wishes, but he must pick up [that one marked silver dollar]. What chance would he have of getting the right one?" Stoner concludes, "Just the same chance the prophets would have had of writing those eight prophecies and having them all come true in any one man ... providing they wrote them in their own wisdom."

## Lunatic, Liar, or Lord

Almost 2,000 years after Jesus' death and Resurrection, it's become common to say that Jesus was a great man or a great moral teacher. But most of the people who make that claim have probably never carefully read the words Jesus spoke. Jesus claimed to speak for God. He said He could forgive sin. He called God His Father. He said He was the "Son of Man," another name for the Messiah. He told the people of Israel, who thought God belonged to them, that God loved all people.

But His most outrageous claim was this: Jesus predicted that He would be arrested, killed, and buried—then, on the third day, He would "be raised to life." (LUKE 9:22) These aren't the words of a good man or a great teacher. They are the words of someone who thinks he's the Son of God.

C.S. Lewis put it this way: "A man who was merely a man and said the sort of things Jesus said would not be a great moral teacher. He would either be a lunatic—on the level with a man who says he is a poached egg—or he would be the devil of hell. You must take your choice. Either this was, and is, the Son of God, or else a madman or something worse. You can shut Him up for a fool or you can fall at His feet and call Him Lord and God. But let us not come with any patronizing nonsense about His being a great human teacher. He has not left that open to us."

Years ago, after finally approaching the evidence for the Resurrection with an open mind, I discovered to my surprise that I now agreed with Canon Westcott from Cambridge University, who stated:

*"Indeed, taking all the evidence together, it is not too much to say that there is no historic incident better or more variously supported than the Resurrection of Christ. Nothing but the antecedent assumption that it must be false could have suggested the idea of deficiency in the proof of it."*

## What If It's True?

Now, what about you? For 31 chapters you have looked at what unleashing the power of the Resurrection can mean for your life. If this book has helped you discover the reality of the Resurrection, and you prayed the same prayer that changed the course of my life, congratulations! This could be the first day of the best of your life.

Or perhaps you are still skeptical. So was I—for a long time. I would encourage you to keep reading, researching, and praying. Ask God to reveal Himself to you. Put this in high gear. A lot is riding on this decision. If the Resurrection is true—and the evidence is compelling—then you can experience God's forgiveness for your past, God's power for your present and God's promises for your future. Why would you want to live any other way?

# ADDITIONAL RESOURCES

# LEADING A SMALL GROUP

WHO, ME? To lead a small group, you don't need to be a scholar, teacher, or theologian, because it's not about lecturing. It's about asking questions and listening. If you love God and like people, you have everything you need to lead a small group. Congratulations!

## Tips on how to lead a small group:

1   **Help people get comfortable.** Most people are comfortable reading, but there are exceptions. The same goes for praying. Take volunteers for these opportunities rather than risk losing someone because they felt pressure to read or pray.

2   **Start with easy questions.** This helps to get people talking. Use questions such as: What does it say? Maybe open the discussion with a "hook"—an observation or question about life in general—with which most everyone can identify. Try to involve everyone in the interaction but don't call on specific people to respond.

3   **Be careful about the use of Christian-ese.** Often, new people don't understand the terms. (They might think that the Sadducees are depressed people, or that epistles were the wives of the apostles.)

4   **Close in prayer.** This helps draw the small group time to an appropriate conclusion.

# SMALL-GROUP DISCUSSION QUESTIONS

## Week One

1   From the six benefits of the Resurrection shared in Chapters
    1–6, which one means the most to you and why?

> Because of the Resurrection, you can:
> Develop a confident faith
> Receive eternal life
> Overcome the odds
> Discover that you matter to God
> Experience a complete transformation
> Live with God's power

2   Read John 20:10–18. Jesus was standing right next to Mary,
    but she didn't recognize Him until He called her name. Can
    any of you share a story of how God got your attention?

3   What do you think are the implications for your life when you
    discover that you matter to God?

4   What noticeable changes have you experienced in your life
    since you received Jesus Christ into your life? What difference
    has it made? Have your family and friends noticed?

5   Share a time in your life when the odds where against you.
    How did God help you overcome those odds?

6   Read Ephesians 1:18-20. God's power is available to all who
    believe in Jesus Christ. Describe what that means to you.

## Week Two

1. From the six benefits of the Resurrection shared in Chapters 7–12, which one means the most to you and why?

> Because of the Resurrection, you can:
> Trust your Bible
> Live with God's joy
> Live with a sense of wonder
> Trust His claims
> Live with God's purpose
> Know God

2. How does living with God's joy affect your life? Does focusing on the truth of the Resurrection add joy to your life even in unfavorable circumstances? Explain.

3. Read Ephesians 2:1–10. According to Paul, what purpose do we live for if we do not have a relationship with Jesus?

4. What does Paul say are the results of a relationship with Jesus? What does verse 10 have to say about our purpose? How can you live that out?

5. Share something that happened when you discovered God's purpose for your life.

6. What do you need to build into your life that would better help you get to know God?

## Week Three

1   From the six benefits of the Resurrection shared in Chapters 13–18, which one means the most to you and why?

> Because of the Resurrection, you can:
> Live with God's guidance and direction
> Live with passion
> Overcome discouragement
> Overcome fear
> Trust His promises
> Change direction

2   What are people in our society passionate about?

3   Discouragement is defined as "the anesthetic that the devil uses on a person just before he reaches in and carves out their heart." Share a discouraging time in your life. How did you overcome the discouragement?

4   If you heard Jesus saying to you, "Don't be afraid," what would that look like in your life today? Explain.

5   Read again the promises in Chapter 17. Share the promise that is most valuable to you today. What difference would trust in that promise make in your life?

6   What will you do to strengthen your trust in Jesus and overcome fear? How can your group help?

## Week Four

1. From the six benefits of the Resurrection shared in Chapters 19–24, which one means the most to you and why?

   Because of the Resurrection, you can:
   - Experience God's presence
   - Stop worrying
   - Let go of guilt
   - Experience real peace
   - Expect great things from God
   - Experience hope

2. *Time* magazine says that we live in "the age of anxiety." Do you agree or disagree? What factors do you think are causing such high levels of anxiety? What impact should a relationship with Christ have on this?

3. Why is guilt such a destructive emotion? Read 1 John 1. What does this passage teach us about God's willingness to forgive?

4. Why do so few Christians dream big? What did you learn from Chapter 23? What dreams do you believe God might have in store for your future?

5. Share a time in your life where God replaced discouragement with hope.

6. In what way, this week will you live out one of the above implications of the Resurrection?

## Week Five

1  From the six benefits of the Resurrection shared in Chapters 25–30, which one means the most to you and why?

> Because of the Resurrection, you can:
> Experience the reality of the cross
> Know God personally
> Receive complete forgiveness
> Know that death is defeated
> Live with eternal values
> Know that Jesus Christ is alive

2  How has knowing God personally changed your life? What kind of things help you develop that relationship?

3  How has God used pain or trouble to help develop your faith and values?

4  Read John 19. Reflect on Jesus' actions and words on the cross. What were His concerns?

5  Think of an illustration to compare the length of our time on earth to the length of eternity. How are you leveraging your life and resources for maximum eternal impact?

6  In Chapter 31, Evidence for the Resurrection, which insights were the most compelling to you and why.

As you finish this study, how would you complete these sentences?

> Because of the Resurrection,
>
> I am…
>
> I can…
>
> I am going to…

# MATERIALS

## Other Books by Ray Johnston

*DevelopingEffectiveLeaders.com*

***Help, I'm a Sunday School Teacher***
Ray Johnston, 1995, Youth Specialties
Zondervan Publishing

Help is on the way in this funny, yet extremely practical, book. Sunday-school veteran Ray Johnston offers sympathy and understanding as he serves up 50 creative ideas you can use to make your Sunday school come alive! Now available in Spanish.

***Developing Student Leaders***
Ray Johnston, 1992, Youth Specialties
Zondervan Publishing

This book provides strategies on how to motivate, select, train, and empower your student leaders to make a difference. It also includes a complete five-week student leadership training course to share with your staff.

***Developing Spiritual Growth in Junior High Students***
Ray Johnston, 1994, Youth Specialties
Zondervan Publishing

Developing spiritual growth in junior high students is not only possible, but essential. This book details reasons why junior high ministry may be the most important thing any church ever invests in. It unpacks 90 different ideas for how to reach, grow, and develop spiritually turned-on junior highers.

## Message Series by Ray Johnston

*DevelopingEffectiveLeaders.com*

### Raising G-Rated Kids in an X-Rated World
- Building Lasting Values in Today's Kids
- Honey, I Shrunk the Kids! 10 Mistakes Parents Make
- 5 Keys to Developing Your Kids
  Spiritual Development, Part 1
- 5 Keys to Developing Your Kids
  Spiritual Development, Part 2

### Truth.com
- Evidence for the Resurrection
- Can I Trust the Bible? Part 1
- Can I Trust the Bible? Part 2
- Is There Evidence for the Existence of God?
- Does Evolution Disprove the Bible? Part 1
- Does Evolution Disprove the Bible? Part 2

### Defeating the Giants in Your Life
- Defeating the Giant of Procrastination
- Defeating the Giant of Loneliness
- Defeating the Giant of Anxiety
- Defeating the Giant of Resentment
- Defeating the Giant of Temptation

### Strengthening Your Family
- Loving Your Marriage Enough to Protect It
- This Year I Will... Quit That Habit
- Love: The Second Time Around
- Parenting to the Max!
- Building Your Marriage to Last a Lifetime!
- Turning Your House Into a Christian Home

### 40 Days of Prayer
- Don't Just Do Something: Sit There!
  Discovering the Power of Prayer
- Why Pray When You Can Worry?
- If at First... Finding Your Way Back From Failure
- Can You Hear Me Now?
- The Power of Praying Together
- 7 Things God Does When You Pray

*Extreme Makeover*
- Experiencing God's Power to Change
- Extreme Makeover—Joy
- Extreme Makeover—Faithfulness
- Extreme Makeover—Patience
- Extreme Makeover—Peace
- Extreme Makeover—Self-Control, Part 1, 2, & 3

*Get in the Game—*
*Discovering and Developing Your Spiritual Gifts*
- Part 1—Introduction
- Part 2—Gifts Defined
- Part 3—How Do I Use My Spiritual Gifts
- Part 4—Fellowship and Task-Oriented Gifts
- Part 5—Support Gifts
- Part 6—Unwrapping Your Gifts
- Part 7—How to be Used by God
- Part 8—Living a Life That Honors God

## Speaking Engagements

Ray Johnston is available to speak at churches and conferences. Please contact his assistant, Cindy Uhler, at (916) 791-1244 or go to DevelopingEffectiveLeaders.com.

## Thrive Conferences

Bayside Church is home to the annual Thrive Conference—for anyone who would like to be renewed, refreshed, and recharged for service in an upbeat, worshipful three-day conference with daily break-out sessions. Please visit Thrive2006.com or Thrive2007.com for details.

## The Bayside Family of Churches

For those who want to learn more about the Bayside Family of Churches, our core values, strategy and ministries, service times, and much, much more, please visit us at: BaysideOnline.com.

# SUGGESTED READING

I SERVE AS A PASTOR OF A CHURCH for people who usually don't like church. We have seen thousands of people move from skepticism to Christianity in the last 12 years. In conversations with former skeptics who have crossed the line of faith, many report the following books have been helpful:

*Did Jesus Rise From the Dead?* Gary R. Habermas and Antony G. N. Flew. San Francisco: Harper & Row, Publishers, 1987

*Who Moved the Stone?* Frank Morison. London: The Century Co., 1930

*The Case for Christ.* Lee Strobel. Grand Rapids: Zondervan, 1998

*The Case for Faith.* Lee Strobel. Grand Rapids: Zondervan, 2000

*The Case for Easter.* Lee Strobel. Grand Rapids: Zondervan, 1998

*Evidence That Demands a Verdict.* Josh McDowell. Nelson Reference, 1992

*A Ready Defense.* Josh McDowell. Nelson Reference, 1992

*More Than a Carpenter.* Josh McDowell. Tyndale House Publishers, 1987

*Letters From a Skeptic.* Gregory A. Boyd. Cook Communications, 2004

*The New Testament Documents: Are They Reliable?* F.F. Bruce. Wm. B. Eerdmans Publishing Co., 2003

*The Reality of the Resurrection.* Merrill C. Tenney. New York: Harper & Row, 1963